D1384231

MURDER

at the

AIRPORT

INN

John L. Young

Copyright © 2004 by John L. Young

Published By

WINDY KNOLL PRODUCTIONS
R. D. # 2, BOX 2204
RUSSELL, PA 16345

Cover Photo: Warren County Historical Society

Back cover author photo: Debra Young

I want to thank and acknowledge those who helped with this book. First, as always, I thank Debra, my wife, editor, and overall helpmate. Next, much thanks to Charlotte Eriksen Hunt—without her keen memory there would have been no book. The Warren County Public Library Research Department has always offered help and guidance, but this time out their assistance was invaluable. Thanks also to the Warren County Historical Society. And finally, thanks to attorney Marsha Ziki for reading my manuscript and making suggestions.

You shall not murder.

EXODUS 20: 13

CHAPTER I

In Warren County, Pennsylvania in the 1920s, people who took an interest in such things were convinced that there was something fishy going on at the Brokenstraw Airport. Either that or it was just plain jinxed. How else could you explain that every time a new owner got the business up and running there would be a mysterious fire and the business would fold? The first time this happened, the fire destroyed the hangars as well as four airplanes and a glider. If this had happened once—or even twice, it could have been passed off as just plain bad luck. But when it happened a third time the legend of the jinx was firmly rooted, albeit when some said the word *jinx* they raised their eyebrows in a knowing disbelief.

For those who didn't believe in the jinx and those who didn't believe in owner hi-jinx, the Brokenstraw Airport was simply one of those unfortunate businesses that just couldn't seem to get off the ground. At any rate, all that was left of the airport when this story begins is the runway, the charred foundations of the hangars, and a two-story, frame house that sat facing the Theodore Roosevelt Highway, also known as U.S. Route 6.

This is what thirty-three-year-old Russian immigrant Metro (pronounced Meetro) Seminuk bought from his older brother Wasel in 1930. Apparently, Metro didn't believe in the jinx. Also, he had different plans than his brother and the previous owners. He would keep his head out of the clouds and his feet on the ground. Instead of another attempt at an airport, he opened a roadhouse: a combination general store, gas station, restaurant, and dance hall, with a second-floor apartment where he and his wife and daughter would live. He named his new business, appropriately enough, the Airport Inn.

Metro was also lucky enough to be in the right business at the right time. On the other hand, the unluckiest business owners in the United States had to be those who made their living from "the manufacture, sale, or transportation of intoxicating liquors" on January 16, 1920. On this day the 18th Amendment to the constitution was voted into existence and Prohibition began. It ended in 1933, just a few years after Metro had set his plans for a roadside tavern into existence.

But despite all of Metro's hard work and the fact that the business was doing well, the jinx would return—with a vengeance—during the waning hours of March 26, 1936.

***

Northwestern Pennsylvania had an illustrious history long before Metro Seminuk and what historians would later call the "first wave" of Europeans immigrated to America. French missionaries and traders, who made their way westward from Quebec and the settlements along the Atlantic Coast in the early 1700s, used the Allegheny River in northwestern Pennsylvania as an avenue of approach to the great Mississippi basin. When they reached the site where the Conewango Creek emptied into the Allegheny River, they discovered evidence of a long-established Iroquois village. The Iroquois used this confluence of waters to launch their canoe expeditions—friendly or warlike.

There are no records of any white settlers having settled permanently in this area of northwestern Pennsylvania prior to 1794. But settlers came and Warren County was established in 1800 and by 1805 there were two-hundred-and-five "white taxables" in Warren County. The area's namesake, General Joseph Warren, was a Harvard graduate and physician who had served with the Patriot Party and the Revolutionary forces until he was killed in action at Bunker Hill on June 17, 1775.

The borough of Warren was established on May 7, 1832 on the very site where the Conewango Creek meets the Allegheny River.

Early settlers to the area were attracted by vast forests of timber—especially the multiple-use white pine, and in no time they had set up sawmills and lumber camps throughout the region. During the early 1800s the lumbering business flourished; there was not only an abundance of timber in Warren County but there was a network of waterways, made up by the Conewango, Kinzua, Brokenstraw, and Jackson Run creeks, whereby logs, made into rafts, were floated to the Allegheny River. At the Allegheny River six or eight of these smaller rafts were spliced together—forming what was known as an "Allegheny," which was then floated downstream to Pittsburgh. In Pittsburgh the Allegheny River met the Monongahela River and formed the Ohio River where the rafts continued westward into Ohio and eventually to the Mississippi River.

Lumbering in Warren County reached its high-water mark during the years leading up to 1840. In 1838 a depression in business followed by the general bank suspension, crippled the lumber industry locally and from then on it gradually diminished. Also, as the prime areas were clear-cut, trees were harder to get to and more importantly harder to get back out. To get around this, workers hauled steam boilers into the forests and set up lumber manufacturing mills onsite; the rough boards—much easier to transport than the mammoth logs, were then transported to local lumber mills or onto rafts on the Allegheny River.

In 1859, however, an event would take place in Venango County, just miles from the southwestern tip of Warren County, that would change northwestern Pennsylvania—and the world—forever: Colonel Edwin Drake drilled the world's first commercial oil well. Seemingly overnight, Warren manufacturing shifted from lumber mills to producing oil products and equipment for the new oilfield industry, which flourished in northwestern Pennsylvania as workers and their families, entrepreneurs, and would-be millionaires flocked to the area by the thousands.

By 1936 the population of the borough of Warren was slightly over 15,000. The population in Warren County was 43,368, of those 9,265 were considered 'rural,' e.g., farmers. The borough comprised an area of over 8 square miles; there were 6 public parks on a total of 69 acres. There were 3 banks with deposits totaling $15,145,807 and total resources of $17,494,338. There were 4,670 homes, 3,950 telephones, 29 churches representing 17 denominations, 1 daily newspaper, 4 hotels, 1 hospital with 100 beds, 1 public library, 9 public schools with 3,175 students and 106 teachers, 1 parochial school with 190 students and 4 teachers.

There were 64 manufacturers that employed 2,478 workers. The principal manufactured products were refined oil, furniture, and steel products.

The fire department had 17 men, 3 stations, and 6 pieces of motor equipment; the police department had 9 men, 1 station, and 3 pieces of motor equipment. The total street mileage was 42.2 miles, 13.7 miles of which were paved. There were 2 railroads: the Pennsylvania and the New York Central, 1 municipal airport, and 2 highways: the state-owned Allegheny Highway, which ran north and south, and the federally owned Theodore Roosevelt Highway, which ran east and west.

***

The United States Weather Bureau declared the winter of 1936 the coldest winter on record. Pennsylvania got hit hard. In many places, the ground was frozen solid up to four feet. From one end of the state to the other, the mountains were covered with snow and ice. Then, on Sunday evening, March 15, it began to rain and it continued without letup for fifty hours. Rivers rose rapidly and overflowed into nearby tributaries, which in turn overflowed their banks. Bridges were either damaged or washed out and railroad lines were closed, damages were racked up into the hundreds of millions of dollars. By March 17, St. Patrick's Day, floodwaters covered most of the state's floodplain areas.

Floodwaters from the Allegheny River inundated the city of Pittsburgh as the waters reached the high water mark of forty-six feet. By March 20, there were forty-five dead, three-hundred-and-fifty confirmed injured, and hundreds—if not thousands—missing in Pittsburgh alone. This, what would become known as the "St.Patrick's Day Flood of 1936," would stand as the worst flood in Pittsburgh's history.

Meanwhile, one-hundred-and-forty-five miles upriver, the borough of Warren and the towns and villages in Warren County had problems of their own. A heavy, wet snowfall, which had begun during the early morning hours of March 17, was coming down at the rate of two to three inches an hour and continued for twenty-four hours straight. The weather turned colder and the rain-like snow turned to sleet. On Saturday, March 21 a second snowstorm swamped the area, raising the two-storm snowfall to a total of forty-four inches.

A few days later, the weather turned warmer. Local streams and their tributaries overflowed their banks as the water flooded the lowlands and made its way to the Allegheny River, which was raging toward Pittsburgh. In Brokenstraw Township, Brokenstraw Creek was over its banks and had flooded the area along U.S. Route 6. In Youngsville, school children who rode the train to their homes in outlying areas were stranded in schools until school officials farmed them out to spend the night with families in Youngsville. Roads were closed and the trolley and railroad lines were shut down. Rescue crews and those who absolutely had to get somewhere went by small boat.

By March 26, the snow was gone and the waters had receded to a negotiable level. Trolleys, trains, and buses were running again. Most of the main roads were open; and although many local roads were open, the mud, left over from the flooding made most of them a slippery mess. And more than one area farmer made a few extra bucks pulling a car out of a roadside ditch with his team of horses.

U.S. Route 6—originally called the Theodore Roosevelt Highway—was four-hundred-miles long and ran from one end of the state to the other. In 1936 it was the Commonwealth's longest highway: it ran across the Allegheny Plateau in western Pennsylvania and across the Northern Tier as it made its way eastward. Along the way it connected the county seats of each county through which it passed. It was improved in 1931 as part of then-Governor Pinchot's plan to expand and improve the state's highway system and "get the farmer out of the mud."

U.S. Route 6 was paved, but on Thursday, March 26, 1936 it was muddy and slippery.

CHAPTER II

Business was slow at the Airport Inn on the night of Thursday, March 26, 1936. In fact for most of the night, aside from one or two men who had slipped in and out for a quick one, Metro had but one customer: a local farmer named Tom Bower. Bower had walked to the bar from his nearby farm, which was a mile south of the Inn at the foot of a hill that was known locally as York Mountain. He'd walked to the bar a number of times but it was such a lousy day, even he might not have been out that night except for the fact that he and his family had no electricity and he had walked to the Airport Inn with his can to get kerosene. Of course he had pumped his kerosene into his can and had set the can outside while he had a drink and a sandwich.

Clearly, the flooding and the muddy roads had discouraged all but the necessary traveler. So when the door to the bar swung open that night around 10:30 both men were surprised to see a lone traveler, a stranger to them both, walk to the bar and order a shot of rye. Tom and Metro had seen the man once before: earlier that day, in the late afternoon, when the stranger had stopped in and asked for directions to Corry, then left quickly.

But tonight the stranger was back and he was all wound up and he felt like talking. The young man, lanky and good-looking, told the men he had been working in New York City and that he was on his way to accept another position. Bower would later tell the authorities, "This stranger was either a most unusual young man or one of the world's worst liars." Bower continued, "The young man began to spin these wondrous tall tales. We didn't know if they were true or not." But, just the same, Bower and Metro listened, after all, there was precious little else to entertain the men that dark and stormy night.

Around 11:45 Metro's twenty-eight-year-old wife Mary passed through the café on her way upstairs to prepare for bed. A few minutes before midnight she called down to her husband, "What time are you closing tonight, dear?"

"Right away," Metro answered. At that point Bower said goodnight and made his way to the door. As he was leaving he heard the stranger ask for a tank of gasoline.

Bower picked up his can of kerosene and walked across Route 6 and was making his way along the tracks of the Pennsylvania Railroad. Between the tracks and the properties that bordered it there was a stretch of overgrown right-of-way, a buffer between the farms that lay in the fields to the south and the raised tracks. Bower had just walked down the gravel slope of the tracks and was about to get on the narrow footpath that ran through the scrub when he heard the shots.

Bower scrambled to the top of the slope and saw Metro slumping to the ground beside the gas pumps and the stranger speeding off in his car, heading west on Route 6. Out of the darkness he heard the upstairs window flung open and he heard Mary screaming down, "Metro! Metro!"

Bower dropped his can and ran back to the gasoline pumps. By the time he got there Mary and her daughter Helen and her mother Dora were already there, screaming and wailing over Metro's body. Mary threw herself onto her husband's motionless body. Bower reached his hand to Metro's chest and felt for the movement of his heart, but there was none.

Bower rushed to phone the police and less than a half-hour later, Sheriff John Berdine and a team of investigators were on the scene. The investigative team was comprised of six men: deputies Ernest Berdine and William Stuart, District Attorney Leroy C. Eddy, Coroner Ed Lowery, and Pennsylvania State troopers Joseph Schmidt and John Mehallick.

"He drove that way," Bower rushed excitedly toward the investigators, with his arm extended pointing westward on Route 6. Bower told the men that the stranger was driving a mud-splattered 1933 or 1934 black Plymouth and that when he left the bar he was curious about the stranger and he had glanced at the stranger's license plate out of curiosity, but it was covered with mud.

Meanwhile, Coroner Lowrey examined the body of Metro Seminuk and discovered three bullet holes: two on the right side of the abdomen and one above the hip. Lowrey would state later that any one of the shots could have killed Seminuk. The official photographer arrived, set up his powerful floodlights and photographed the body, while investigators combed the driveway for any possible evidence the perpetrator may have accidentally left behind. They found nothing and within an hour the body was removed and the driveway search was called off.

Sheriff Berdine immediately called the State Police to set up roadblocks on Route 6. State Police Corporal Joseph Schmidt took Mary inside and questioned her and her mother, Mrs. Dora Zurkan, the latter having said she had been asleep upstairs when she heard the shots.

Despite her reddened eyes and disheveled hair, Schmidt noted that, with her bobbed blonde hair and thin figure, Mary Seminuk was an attractive woman. His questioning was interrupted when Mary and Metro's eleven-year-old daughter Helen called to her mother from upstairs and Mary went upstairs to get her settled. When she returned downstairs, Corporal Schmidt continued the questioning.

"Did you ever see this man before?" Schmidt asked regarding the young stranger.

"I did," Mary responded. Then she related that she had seen the stranger when she had passed through the bar on her way upstairs earlier that night.

"Did your husband know any people who wished him harm?" Schmidt continued.

At this question Mary hesitated, looked at the floor then responded, "No."

"Then why did you hesitate with your answer?" Schmidt asked.

Mary let out slowly, "During Prohibition, Metro was part of a gang that ran beer across the Great Lakes from Canada into this country." She hesitated again then added, "If he did have an enemy from those days, I swear I couldn't give you a name because I don't know any."

Mary's suspicions about a possible enemy of her husband's from his alleged rum-running days pulling the trigger were not far-fetched. In Great Lakes port cities, such as Buffalo and Erie, rumrunners, who smuggled alcohol from Canada (where it was legal to produce) to the United States, had a ready market for their illicit cargo. In fact, bootlegging became the cash crop of America's newest enterprise, the "Underworld" of gangsters. From Al Capone in Chicago all the way down to smalltime fishermen and "gin joint" operators, bootlegging earned big bucks for those who were willing to get involved.

Metro had been known to regularly drive to Erie. And in the days of Prohibition (1920-1933), downtown Erie, especially the area that grew out from the docks, was a rough-and-tumble neighborhood where anything—including murder—could happen. The most famous—or infamous—case was the murder of Fred Moran on January 17, 1921—just one day past the year that Prohibition had been in effect.

Moran was a forty-two-year-old married alderman who was "shot in a drunken brawl at a house of ill fame." Moran was seen by many of Erie's law-abiding residents as the connecting link between Official Life and the Underworld of Erie. The Moran murder understandably made big news when it was pointed out that the deceased was "carrying on a highly visible love affair with the black proprietress of a brothel."

The Moran murder case eventually led to an investigation into the city's government, starting at the top with Mayor Kitts. In all, a grand jury indicted forty-three officials including Police Chief William Dentzel and thirty-one of his officers. Clearly, the city of Erie was a hotbed of criminal activity that centered around rum running and bootlegging.

The question then became: Before Prohibition ended had Metro Seminuk been buying illegal booze in Erie and transporting it back to his roadhouse to sell? Had he made an enemy in the Erie Underworld? Did he make the one-hour drive to Erie to get his share of the American Dream and end up with a nightmare?

If he did, he wasn't the only businessman to get caught up in bootlegging. There was no shortage of honest, hardworking Americans who were seduced into the world of fast money that Prohibition provided. In port cities like Erie, sometimes it was the local fishermen who supplied the craft and the cunning and the daring to make the run twenty-two miles across Lake Erie to Long Point, Ontario and back. Most of these trips were done at night, under the cover of darkness. And sometimes, their Canadian counterparts would bring the stash just so far out into the lake so that they were still in Canadian waters and the American skipper would have to find these small boats—not an easy thing to do unless you had years of experience on the lake.

One local fisherman, who had no intention of joining the Underworld, tells the story that he was at the local fisheries when a man came to him and asked him if he would go out and tow in his vessel which had broken down on the lake. The man gave the fisherman the general whereabouts of the boat and the fisherman was able to go right to it and bring it in safely. The man was highly impressed and gave the fisherman $100 for his trouble. But then he added that he would give the fisherman $100 a trip for each load of illegal booze he brought across.

"I was working for a dollar a day and board," the fisherman told an interviewer years later for the book "Lake Erie Fishermen," which was, as the title suggests, a collection of tales from Lake Erie fishermen. "Then when I got married I got fifteen dollars a week. That's what I was making when I started running whisky. I bring over a load worth about ten-thousand dollars and I'd get one-hundred dollars."

Erie court dockets from the Prohibition period show that Erie had its share of wanna-be-bootleg czars—both on the lake and on land. Many of those who got caught did very little jail time. Most were sentenced to four months in the Erie County Jail and were fined $500 plus court costs, for a grand total of $536. The standard charge in Erie County for bootleggers read "Unlawful possession of intoxicating liquor, for beverage purposes."

Reading through the trial transcripts, I soon realized that the trials were more-or-less perfunctory. The procedure was strictly boilerplate. It became easy to picture the accused standing beside his attorney with his hat in his hand and his head slightly bowed: "Yes, your honor. Yes, your honor." And the judge: quickly reading the sentence, slamming his gavel as he called out "Next."

But every now and then a case came along with a little different spin on it. Take the case of Rafaello Saraceno. On January 3, 1924 Saraceno was brought before the court and charged with "unlawful transportation." It seems he was making his deliveries in his truck when the police found him with forty-one one-gallon cans of alcohol. Just as all the other bootleggers Saraceno got the standard four month sentence and a $500-fine and he got his alcohol confiscated.

His court docket reads: "Said intoxicating liquor is hereby adjudged forfeited and condemned and Sheriff of Erie County is directed to deliver twenty gallons to Soldiers & Sailors Home, ten gallons to Hamot Hospital, and eleven gallons to St. Vincent Hospital."

Saraceno was also charged with carrying a concealed weapon but that charge went away when the prosecutor claimed *"nolle prosequi,"* which in plain English meant he was dropping all or part of the indictment.

But as the 1920s turned into the 1930s and the Great Depression took hold, more and more Americans and elected officials grew tired of Prohibition. They were disillusioned that the government had failed to enforce Prohibition and many blamed Prohibition for the loss of jobs and loss of revenue for state and federal government. As a result Congress passed the 21st Amendment which repealed the 18th Amendment and Prohibition in December 1933.

But the Port of Erie had been the landing site of another type of smuggling, even before Prohibition, and, as would come up later in this story, Metro Seminuk was accused of being part of this smuggling ring as well.

During the early part of the 20th Century, a movement began in the United States that wanted to stem the flow of immigrants from Southern and Eastern Europe (and other countries). The first wave of these immigrants were Poles, Slovaks, Hungarians, and Russians. Because of the ongoing border wars and shifting political alliances formed, the U.S. Immigration Service many times listed immigrants from these countries as Ukrainians, regardless of which country they were from. During the period from 1870 to 1914, immigration records show that roughly 500,000 "Ukrainians" immigrated to America.

In response to the growing opinion that there were too many unwanted immigrants making their way to the United States, Congress passed the Quota Act of 1921, followed by the even more restrictive Johnson-Reed Immigration Act of 1924. Using a formula skewed to favor those immigrants that were deemed "desirable," these measures provided the following annual quotas, beginning in 1924. Germany was allowed the most with slightly over 50,000; Great Britain and Northern Ireland, 34,000; Ireland 28,000. By contrast, eastern and southern European countries: Poland, 5,900; Italy, 3,800; Russia, 2,200; Lithuania, 344; Bulgaria, 100, and so on.

Meanwhile, life in Southern and Eastern Europe became more and more repressive as governing countries sought to force their agendas and propaganda onto the populace. Many sought asylum in the United States and when those borders were closed, some immigrated to Canada to await immigration to the United States. And when the wait became too long, or, for one reason or another, their immigration to the U.S. was denied, some were smuggled across Lake Erie from Ontario, Canada to Buffalo and Erie, using the same routes and even the same vessels as the rum-runners.

Was Metro Seminuk part of this clandestine operation? If he was buying beer and whisky illegally from Erie rum-runners, would it be a natural assumption that he would earn a few extra dollars by bringing his fellow countrymen into the U.S.? Metro did speak and read Russian. (Mary Seminuk was of Rumanian descent. Her parents had first immigrated to Canada, legally, before coming to the Unites States and getting their citizenship.)

At any rate, later in this story, Metro would be accused of being involved in smuggling and other illegal activities.

CHAPTER III

During his questioning on the night of Metro Seminuk's murder, Tom Bower described the suspect as medium height, about thirty, good-looking with sandy hair, parted on the side. Bower said the young man told him his name was Gerald Chapman. The investigators thought it odd that one of the country's most infamous criminals—who had recently been apprehended and hanged in Connecticut—was also named Gerald Chapman.

"That young man bragged that he made over $300 a week with Continental Steel in New York City," Bower offered when it was his turn to be questioned. "He said that when they refused to give him a raise, he quit and was on his way now to getting a better job—one with a future."

When investigators asked Bower if he could think of any reason why anyone would want to kill Seminuk, he answered that he did not. He said that Metro was a good guy and treated everyone well.

"How did you get along with your husband?" Schmidt went back again to Mary.

"Like the ordinary married couple I imagine," Mary answered.

"What do you mean by that?" Schmidt kept on.

"We had very few money problems. The Inn is making money, but we had the usual squabbles between husband and wife. About four years ago I didn't think Metro was paying enough attention to the house and I went down to an attorney to file suit for a divorce, but that was all that was needed to make Metro come around nicely. Since then we have had no trouble."

13

"Have you been happy together?" Schmidt asked
"Very happy," Mary responded.

CHAPTER IV

Across Route 6 and just across the railroad tracks that ran along-side Route 6, Emilie Eriksen was in the kitchen of her farmhouse when she heard the shots fired that appeared to be coming from the direction of the Airport Inn. Mrs. Eriksen and her husband and nine children had moved into the large farmhouse just a year earlier. The Eriksens weren't doing well. Mr. Eriksen suffered from rheumatoid arthritis and was unable to work, so the responsibility of raising and providing for the couple's nine children fell on Emilie's shoulders.

The family had moved from one impoverished situation to another. Their most recent stay was at Emilie's sister's home in Starbrick. But with the move to the small farm that had a barn and room for a garden, the family's hopes were high. The rent was $12 a month and their landlord, Metro Seminuk, was a friendly and likable guy, who had even used his truck to help the family move in. And although one of Emilie's daughters, Charlotte, was a few years older than Helen Seminuk, the two girls were close enough in age that they did most things together. In fact, just a week earlier on the twenty-second of March, Charlotte had attended Helen's eleventh birthday party at the Airport Inn.

***

With nothing to go on regarding Mary and Metro's marriage, the investigators turned to the physical evidence in the case. When Bower pointed out that the glass the suspect had used was still sitting on the bar, Corporal Schmidt stuck two fingers inside the glass and held it to the light. There were prints of the thumb and two fingers; these would be photographed and the plate taken to the FBI fingerprint lab in Washington, D.C. for comparison with the known criminals in its master files. A match—if there were a match—would be a simple procedure. If indeed there were another criminal named Gerald Chapman, they would soon know.

The next day, Friday, March 27, the *Warren Times Mirror* ran this front-page heading: "IDENTITY OF KILLER UNKNOWN" and below that "Police puzzled by wanton shooting." The article recapped the events of the previous night and stated there was no apparent motive and no robbery.

That same day at the Hull Funeral Home, Dr. M.V. Ball performed the autopsy of Metro Seminuk, wherein he extracted three slugs from a .38 caliber handgun thought to be an Army special.

Meanwhile, the investigation into the character of Metro Seminuk produced the profile of a man whom acquaintances agreed was mild-mannered and intelligent. And, in spite of his alleged rum-running history, he'd had no brushes with the law. Also that day, in response to a telegram sent the night before, Continental Steel responded to local authorities that no one named Gerald Chapman had ever worked for them.

On Saturday, March 28, 1936 the funeral for Metro Seminuk was held at 3 o'clock at the Airport Inn. Fourteen-year-old Charlotte Eriksen went to the funeral.

"I remember Metro's body was laid out in the dance hall. Metro's sister, Katherine Teconchuk, had made tallow candles and she had them placed everywhere," Charlotte Eriksen Hunt explains all these years later. "Mary served hamburgers and at one point her stomach growled and she and her father Nick Zurkan laughed. I remember that I didn't like it that she had laughed."

Katherine Teconchuk's daughter Ruth, now Ruth Teconchuk Scheidermantle, still has vivid memories of her uncle's funeral: "I remember the candles all around and my Uncle Metro's body laid out in the dance hall."

As police continued their search, a man driving through Youngsville was stopped by Deputy Sheriff William Stuart on a traffic violation. When he failed to produce his driver's license he was considered a suspect in the Seminuk murder and brought to the sheriff's office. However, after being questioned and identified by local merchants as a travelling salesman, the man was cleared of any involvement and released.

At this point investigators were stumped. They simply didn't have a motive for the killing. At one point they looked into Metro's life insurance policies, which named Mary as the sole beneficiary; but because they were written for such small amounts—$300 on one and $1,000 on another—it didn't seem likely that money was the motive.

Meanwhile, things were tense at the Teconchuck home on Old Route 6. "My mother was afraid," Ruth said. "This was just days after the killing and we didn't know who had done it. Those were tough times and there were twelve children in our family so my father made moonshine during Prohibition and he was afraid Metro's murder may have been connected to the moonshine. He quit the moonshine business for good after the murder."

It was at this stage in the investigation that Corporal Schmidt and Sheriff Berdine concluded that, as there was no immediate motive, they felt the murder had to be a planned killing. They needed to expand the investigation.

When investigators threw a wider net, they caught their first break in the case in the form of seventeen-year-old Gertrude Manelik, a former waitress at the Airport Inn. She told investigators that the Seminuks had fought over Mary having an affair with a man named John Polens, a former justice of the peace from Garland. With that information in hand, things soon fell in place. Like lined-up dominoes falling once the first domino is set in motion, friends, family members, and neighbors now came forward confirming the fact that Mary and John Polens were indeed an item. One relative of Metro's told of trips the pair had taken to Cleveland and Erie while Metro was a patient at Warren General Hospital for treatment of a rupture.

Investigators went back to the Airport Inn to question Mary about Polens.

"Mrs. Seminuk," Corporal Schmidt started out, "I feel you haven't told the entire truth in this matter."

Mary was more composed this day. The officers noted that the shock of her husband's death had worn off rather quickly.

"Are you inferring that I lied?" Mary raised a penciled eyebrow.

"You told me that your married life with your husband was a happy one. That wasn't exactly the truth, was it?"

17

"I don't know what you mean by happy," Mary countered. "I guess we were as happy as ordinary couples. Of course we had our foolish squabbles."

"Would you call it a foolish squabble when your husband objected to your lover, John Polens?"

"How dare you!" Mary raised her voice in indignation. But after a heated round of questions she burst into tears and admitted that John Polens was a "dear friend."

From there it was a short journey for the officers, both geographically and logically, to the home of thirty-year-old John Polens in nearby Garland. Polens immediately denied the affair and any involvement in Metro's murder. Polens said he couldn't have been the killer because he had spent the entire evening of March 26 at the Garland Inn in the company of two women: Mrs. Mae Clancy and her sister, Margaret Johnson. The sisters confirmed his story adding that he did not leave the bar until well after midnight. Polens' story was further confirmed when he was brought back to Warren and put before Tom Bower and Bower said Polens was not the stranger in the bar that night.

But as a result of repeated questioning, Polens did admit that he and Mary had taken a number of "chaperoned" overnight trips to Buffalo, Cleveland, and Erie.

At this point—three days after the murder—Corporal Schmidt realized that the only probable motive in the case was the love triangle created by the affair of John Polens and Mary Seminuk. Yet, based solely on what he had learned so far, he did not have any evidence against the pair. It was then that he realized that the investigators had to go back to the physical evidence. They had to find the getaway car; they had to find the black Plymouth.

Schmidt was still puzzled how the Plymouth had managed to escape the roadblocks that had been set up that night. If the suspect had pulled off Route 6 onto a secondary road, it was almost certain he would have trouble negotiating the floodwaters and the mud. It was then that Investigator Schmidt remembered that Bower had said that the suspect told him the reason his pants were so muddy was because he had slid off the road and a farmer had pulled him out of the ditch with his team of horses. Schmidt gathered his men and directed them to canvas the farms in the area to see if any farmer had pulled a car out of a ditch on the day of the murder.

The men fanned out. No matter how long it took or how wearying it would be to trudge through the mud, they had their instructions. They were going to visit every farmhouse in the area.

Ruth Scheidermantle recalls this part of the investigation: "I'll always remember seeing the detectives make their way to our house in a little boat. Where we lived it was still flooded."

The investigators encountered a few farmers who had indeed pulled a car out of a ditch, but upon further investigation, none of these leads panned out. But before the day was over, the mud-covered investigators learned firsthand the value of basic police work.

The break came when detectives questioned a farmer named Mike Kowalski, whose farm was in Spring Creek Township, just east of the Erie County line. He told investigators he had hitched up his team and pulled a dark Plymouth sedan out of a ditch. He continued that the car belonged to a young fellow named Joe Sennette, and that Sennette, who wasn't there at the time, was staying at the farm while he visited Kowalski's daughter Katherine.

At two-thirty that afternoon, Sennette returned to the Kowalski farm and was immediately taken into custody by the Corry Police who delivered him to Corporal Schmidt for questioning.

"I don't see how you guys caught up with me so soon," Sennette shook his head, "but I guess I might as well admit everything."

To that Schmidt replied, "That's the smartest thing you can do."

Sennette fit the description all right: sandy hair, medium build, regular features, even good-looking. When asked why he did it, he said he had his reasons.

"Must have been pretty strong reasons if they led you to murder," Schmidt said.

"Murder!" Sennette exclaimed. He said that he hadn't murdered anybody: He was referring to the jam he'd gotten himself into in Cleveland. He said he had jumped bail on an assault charge and had come to this area to stay with Katherine Kowalski and lay low for a while. [It would also come out later in the investigation that Sennette was wanted for questioning in Pittsburgh for the theft of an 800-lb. safe and $18,000 in cash and valuables from the home of Albert J. Kubanek.]

If Sennette fancied himself to be the next Gerald Chapman, he was a dismal failure. As a criminal, Sennette had a lot to learn. In no time, investigators at the Kowalski farm had searched the house and grounds and found a .38 caliber Army special in a manure pile. Officer Mehallick rushed the weapon to Schmidt's office where Schmidt confronted Sennette with the cold, hard reality that in addition to the fact that Sennette matched Tom Bower's description, the police knew about the Plymouth and had found the pistol. There was one other irrefutable piece of evidence. The murderer had left his fingerprints on a glass at the bar.

"I guess you're right," the young man said. "You were bound to catch up with me sooner or later. I killed him."

CHAPTER V

Although Sennette's confession shocked Corporal Schmidt, he still didn't have a motive. He needed to know why Sennette shot Metro Seminuk. It was at this stage of the investigation—for reasons known only to himself—that Sennette decided to open up. He admitted that John Polens had paid him to kill Metro Seminuk. He said it all started when he got in trouble in Cleveland and was out on bail and he met Katherine Kowalski, who invited him to a New Year's Eve party. He skipped bail and came to the area to stay at the Kowalski farm.

At the party he met John Polens, who asked him if he knew any racketeers in Cleveland that he could hire to kill a guy. During the conversation, Polens asked him if he would do the job. Polens said that he'd pay him the same money as he would a hit man.

In early March Polens gave Sennette $50 as a down payment. On March 26, the day of the murder, Polens drove Sennette to a Buffalo car rental, where they rented the Plymouth. On the way back, they stopped and Polens gave Sennette the .38 caliber Army special pistol and instructed him to take a few practice shots into the nearby trees.

They stopped a second time and Polens bought a bottle of liquor. Then they drove slowly past the Airport Inn so that Polens could point it out as the place where Seminuk would be tending bar that night. At 8:30 that night they met at the Garland Inn for drinks and smoked two marijuana cigarettes, after which Sennette left and drove to the Airport Inn.

Sennette admitted Polens had paid him a total of $200 in three payments. He admitted also that his name was not Joe Sennette, that he used the aliases of John Kowalski, Gerald Chapman, Joe Goldberg, and Joseph Sonetti. His real name, he said, was Joseph Senauskas. Investigator Schmidt now knew a great deal about the murder. But one question remained: What did Mary Seminuk have to do with the murder? Senauskas answered that all he knew was that Polens was stuck on Mary and wanted Metro out of the way.

Meanwhile, John Polens had fled the area and was staying with relatives on Travella Avenue in Pittsburgh. Investigators went to Pittsburgh and after a short car chase stopped him and advised him that they were taking him back to Warren. Polens quickly reached for an inside coat pocket but police grabbed him before he had time to produce the .32 caliber pistol he had stashed there for just such emergencies. Polens was returned to Warren County and brought before Schmidt for questioning. At first he denied any involvement but as Schmidt reviewed the evidence in the case, Polens' resolve weakened. At this point Corporal Schmidt said to him the same thing he had said to Senauskas: "If you tell me the truth, I will speak to District Attorney Eddy on your behalf."

Polens admitted his part and made a full written confession. But he added a new twist. He stated that the murder was in self-defense; he stated that Seminuk had threatened his life. He denied that Mary Seminuk had been his mistress, but when asked where he got the money, he replied, "From Mary Seminuk."

It was during this time that investigators questioned fourteen-year-old Charlotte Eriksen.

"I was out carrying wood in when a car pulled up and a police-man asked me 'Are you Charlotte?'

"I answered, 'Yes, I'm Charlotte.'"

"Then he asked me if I'd ever seen Mary with Polens. I had to say yes. I told him that I went to the Airport Inn every morning to pick up the milk for our family. I told him that Mary and Metro were very nice to me, but that I had seen Mary and Polens embracing one day by the oil stove. I walked in and there they were.

"Polens jumped back and got real excited—I always thought he was a wimp, anyway. Then Mary said, 'Don't worry, it's only Charlotte.'"

On April 7 Senauskas and Polens were arraigned at the Warren County Courthouse in front of President Judge Delford U. Arird. The courtroom was standing-room-only, as curious residents and reporters from newspapers across the state came to get a look at the alleged killers.

In April of 1936 Judge Arird was one month shy of his eighty-fifth birthday. A lifelong bachelor, he made his home with his niece Miss Alice Mead, whose home was in the Crescent Park section of Warren.

Judge Arird was born May 21, 1851 in Sugar Grove. After graduation from the Collegiate Institution in Jamestown, New York he became a schoolteacher and eventually principal of Union Schools in Youngsville. He was admitted to the Bar in 1892 and in 1922 he was elected President Judge of the 37th Judicial District, which was comprised of Warren and Forest counties. He held this position until he retired in 1941. He died four years later on January 17, 1945 and is buried alongside his niece in the Youngsville Cemetery.

To add to the excitement of the trials, on April 11 a Russian immigrant from Erie, whose name was being withheld, came forward to the State Police and stated that he knew Senauskas was the killer. He said that Metro had even been warned, and that he—the Russian—even knew about Polens and Senauskas taking target practice.

On April 13, Tom Bower positively identified Joe Senauskas as the killer. Police released information that Joe Senauskas was the man Bower identified and that Senauskas had admitted to police that he used a number of aliases, including Joe Sennette and Gerald Chapman.

By April 14, the hearing for John Polens was in progress. At the hearing, Tom Bower testified that on the night of the murder Senauskas sat at a table in the Airport Inn and drank beer and whiskey for about an hour.

During this period, investigators continued questioning Mary Seminuk about her role in the killing. As a result of these interrogations Mary and her mother, Dora Zurkan, were arrested on May 13 as material witnesses and held on $3,000 bond each. Mary was being held for complicity because she had given Polens money. Police added yet another twist at this time. They stated that their suspicions about Mary heated up even more when it was learned that just days after the murder Mary sold the Airport Inn and 30 acres of property to a man named Victor Nelson for $5,500.

Within four days of her arrest Mary Seminuk was being held over without bail until she would appear before the Grand Jury.

There was only one witness at Mary's Grand Jury hearing, which began May 26. State Police Private John Mehallick testified that he had questioned Mary on two different occasions: on April 10 for four hours and for three hours the next morning. He said that Mary told him that she and Metro had been married twelve years and that they'd had marital difficulties and that Metro had threatened to kill her last summer.

The problem, Mary had told him, was that Metro was receiving anonymous letters regarding her and Polens. She said she first met Polens when he stopped for gas at the Airport Inn in 1931 and that she purchased milk from his Garland dairy farm. She added that over the years she and Polens had "numerous business and friendly calls."

Mary said things came to a boil the previous fall at a dance at the Airport Inn. She and Polens were dancing and Metro separated them, saying to Polens, "If you can't talk to me, you can't talk to my wife."

Then two months prior to the hearing, there was another confrontation. Mary testified that Polens had come to the Airport Inn and Metro and his friends had said something then left; then Polens left and returned shortly and said, "It can be fixed so that they won't talk anymore." She said she believed Polens was talking about a way to stop the anonymous letters.

Mary then offered to furnish the money to "get someone to do away with Metro Seminuk." She said she had originally given Polens $50 around Thanksgiving or Christmas and sometime later another $30 then $100 two days after Metro was discharged from Warren General Hospital, where he had been a patient.

Mary's case went before the jurors on June 1. Judge E.S. Lindsey had been sworn in as special assistant to the district attorney to prosecute the Mary Seminuk, Polens, and Senauskas cases. Attorney A. Lincoln Cohen, from Pittsburgh, would represent Mary and Polens while Earle V. MacDonald of Warren would represent Senauskas.

The next two days, June 2 and 3, turned out to be perhaps the two most important days in the trials of Senauskas and Polens, and one of the most confusing episodes in Warren County jurisprudence. The headline in the *Warren Times Mirror* read: JUDGE & DA MISTAKE DEFENDANT'S PLEA AS GUILTY INSTEAD OF NOT GUILTY.

The first day in court began with the trial of Joe Senauskas, who remained calm during the proceedings and at one point even laughed with his attorney. Senauskas, who said he was born November 21, 1916 in Hartford Connecticut, was described as well dressed and despite his jailhouse pallor, was a rather good-looking young man.

One courthouse reporter wrote, "From the actions of the DA and the officers of the court on June second it appeared a guilty plea was expected and all seemed somewhat surprised when Senauskas changed his plea to not guilty and asked for a trial by jury."

Now the story takes another twist. It's the next day, June 3 and Senauskas' plea of not guilty is still in effect. The jurors were being chosen, but after five jurors were seated, Senauskas abruptly changed his plea to guilty. At this time Judge Arird questioned Senauskas at length, until his attorney Earle V. McDonald objected and brought a halt to the questioning. The five jurors were released and Judge Arird announced that sentencing would be deferred until a later date.

In yet another twist, after Judge Arird accepted Senauskas' plea of guilty, he announced that a hearing would be held at a later date to "determine the degree of the murder." The term "degree of murder" would come to play a critical role in the unfolding drama.

The Senauskas hearing ended at 11 o'clock and Senauskas was escorted by state police back to his cell in the Warren County Jail. Immediately after the noon recess, Polens was brought into court with his attorney L. C. Cohen and he pleaded guilty. Just as swiftly as they had begun, the trials of nineteen-year-old Senauskas and thirty-year-old Polens were over; all that remained was for the judge to pass the sentences.

Mary Seminuk was brought in next. She was wearing a flimsy beige dress, white gloves and no hat. Her face looked thinner and wan compared to her appearance at the time of her hearing. Mary pleaded not guilty. Planning for a long jury selection, the sheriff's department began the selection of an additional fifty names and began the subpoena process. In all, a juror pool of one-hundred-and-fifty persons was almost exhausted; most of the excused admitted they already had an opinion about the trial and still others said they didn't believe in capital punishment. In the end Mary's jury turned out to be comprised of six men and six women.

Mary's trial began at 1:40 on the afternoon of Wednesday, June 3. It began with the coroner and doctors and officials setting the background of the case; there were maps and diagrams of the Airport Inn, photos of the crime scene, and the autopsy report. Every seat in the courtroom was taken as Judge Arird explained that Mary was being tried as an "accessory before the fact," and that she would be tried the same as the person who committed the crime. The DA was charging her with "murder in the first degree."

On June 4, the *Warren Times Mirror* ran this headline: DEATH VERDICT ASKED FOR MRS. SEMINUK.

Before the trial began the next day, Friday, June 5, a stillness covered the courtroom as Mary's eleven-year-old daughter Helen was led to the defense table for a brief visit with her mother. Fourteen-year-old Charlotte Eriksen was in court that day; she and her mother Emilie had been subpoenaed to attend the trial.

Charlotte Eriksen Hunt recalls: "My mother and I had been subpoenaed and attended Mary's trial. Neither of us was ever called to testify, but I was scared just the same. I sat there every day with my mother biting my fingernails. The day Helen was brought in I cried. I went home crying."

With startling clarity Charlotte remembers what she felt about some of the courthouse players during the trial: "I was unimpressed with Cohen. He was a wimp. Judge Arird, I felt, was just plain cocky and smug."

After Helen was led out, the trial began with Gertrude Manelik, the seventeen-year-old waitress who had worked at the Airport Inn. She testified for the prosecution that once at a dance at the Airport Inn, John Polens and Mary were dancing and an argument ensued with Mary's husband Metro. The next witness was Peter Teconchuk who testified to seeing Mary and John Polens together on different occasions.

Pennsylvania State Trooper John Mehallick testified next. He stated that during questioning Mary told him that she had paid Polens to kill her husband. Mehallick walked the jury through the anonymous letters that Mary had told him about and Mary's allegation that Metro had threatened to kill her the previous summer.

Mae Clancy of Garland testified next. She stated that Polens was at the Garland Inn with her and her sister Margaret Johnson on the night of the murder from 7 p.m. until about midnight. She added that she saw Senauskas come into the Garland Inn between 8:30 and 9 p.m. and that he stayed about five minutes; then he returned at 12:15 or 12:30 and inquired after Polens.

Next, fingerprint experts from the Butler and Harrisburg Barracks of the State Police testified that they had examined a fingerprint lifted from a glass at the Airport Inn; and that that print matched Joe Senauskas. H. Rocklin, operator of Thomas Auto Rental in Buffalo, testified that on March 26 he rented a Plymouth to Senauskas and Polens; and that Senauskas returned it the next day at 4:17 p.m., having driven it three-hundred-and-seventy-four miles.

Tom Bower, the farmer who had spent the night of the murder at the Airport Inn drinking with Senauskas, gave his testimony. He identified Senauskas as the young stranger he had drank with and talked with that night. The next witness called was Paul Conklin. He testified that he had stopped briefly at the Airport Inn earlier on the night of the murder and he identified Senauskas as the young stranger he had seen. Conklin added that when he was there he also saw Bower, Metro and Mary Seminuk and Mary's mother, Dora Zurkan.

In an effort to support his assertion that the love triangle of Metro, Mary, and John Polens was at the core of the case, District Attorney Eddy presented a total of six witnesses who at one time or another had seen Mary and Polens together. Sidney Potocki of Erie testified that Mary and Polens had been visitors at his home on two occasions and that on one of those occasions he and Mary and Polens had gone to a beer garden and drank until 1 a.m.

Stanley Osiecki also of Erie testified that he had seen Mary and Polens together. Next, Bertha Karatho testified that the pair had visited her home. Mrs. Anna Seminuk, widow of Metro's brother, testified that she had seen Mary and Polens together on numerous occasions. In fact, she said, she had seen them in a car parked near the Swedish church in Youngsville and Polens had his arm around Mary. Mrs. Seminuk's daughter—also named Anna—corroborated her mother's story. Finally, Metro Manelik testified that he had visited the Airport Inn during the time when Metro was in the hospital and he had observed Mary and Polens together at the Inn.

Mary was then sworn in and she took the stand. She denied all the accusations against her and stated that she was sick at the time of the confession to Officer Mehallick and that she was forced to sign the confession.

Mary stated that she had known John Polens since 1931. She said that she and her husband Metro had had a terrible quarrel in 1931 or 1932 when she found out that he had been a bootlegger. She said that Metro threatened her, "If you don't keep quiet [about the bootlegging] I'll kill you!"

Mary denied she was in love with John Polens. She said of the money that she had given him that $50 was to take care of trouble she was having with the Airport Inn's beer license. And that the remaining $100 was to hire someone to investigate the source of the anonymous letters Metro had been receiving and for the purchase of two automobile tires.

When the issue of her signed confession came up a second time, she repeated that she had been sick when questioned at the courthouse. She admitted that she had turned down the offer of seeing a doctor at the courthouse, stating that she preferred to see her own doctor. She again denied that she knew the money she had given Polens was for a murder plot.

She stated a second time that she had not read her signed confession and that the officers who were questioning her hadn't read it to her. She said the officers told her that if she signed it she could go home; if she didn't sign it she would be sent to jail.

Mary said she had two life insurance policies on Metro. One was for $350 with Polish National Alliance of Chicago and a second policy for $1,000 with Ohio National Life Insurance Company, which they had taken out on February 17, just days before Metro was admitted to Warren General Hospital for a major operation. She also admitted that at one point in their marriage she had started to divorce Metro. But, she added, as a result of her threatening divorce he changed for the better and she dropped the divorce action.

As far as John Polens was concerned, Mary said that she'd had no improper relations with him. The prosecution closed its case at 9:30 a.m.

That afternoon the trial suffered one of its many odd moments when A. Lincoln Cohen, Mary's attorney—and more importantly John Polens' attorney—said in court "that although Senauskas and Polens may be guilty, there is no credible evidence linking Mary to the crime."

Cohen continued, saying that Mary's signed confession was obtained by force; that there was no actual proof of a clandestine love affair with Polens; and that Polens himself had testified that very morning—for the defense—that there was no love affair.

Mary stated again that the money she had given Polens was for auto tires and for him to hire a private investigator. At this point, Judge Arird asked Mary had Polens purchased the tires. Mary answered that she didn't know because she had not seen Polens since she gave him the money. At this point, Cohen called Polens' brother, Gabriel Polens of

Pittsburgh to the stand.

Gabriel Polens testified that on April 3 his brother John Polens gave him $136 to buy tires from E.B. Ashley of Pittsburgh. Ashley took the stand and testified that Gabriel Polens called him on April 3 regarding the purchase of tires. The next witness was William Fider. Fider testified that he had ordered tires from the Airport Inn in February or March and that he had subsequently received the tires, for which he paid $6.50 for two tires and one tube.

Cohen then called John Suda of Brokenstraw Township as a character witness for Mary. Many in attendance, and those who knew Suda, including fourteen-year-old Charlotte Eriksen, questioned the wisdom of putting Suda on the stand.

"John Suda was like an eccentric, like a village idiot. He talked funny and he dressed funny," Charlotte Eriksen Hunt relates. John Suda was born in Russia in 1893. He was, however, Polish and he and his wife spoke Polish. At the time of the trial, the couple had seven children.

Suda testified that he was present when Mary Seminuk objected to Metro purchasing the $1,000 life insurance policy. After his statement, some courtroom spectators snickered and some even laughed out loud.

Judge Arird slammed his gavel and admonished the spectators for their behavior. "This is too serious a crime," Arird chided.

Then, in what can only be termed the next peculiar happening in this trial, Arird made this pronouncement: "The Court is not to blame for having a clown on the witness stand."

When the defense resumed they called Dr. Joseph McCrory, Mary's dentist from Youngsville. He took the stand and testified that Mary had a good reputation.

In an effort to show that Mary and Polens were not lovers—by producing Polens' actual lover—Attorney Cohen then called Mrs. June Bryce of Garland. Mrs. Bryce testified that she had been dating Polens for the last six months and that she and he were "very friendly." The prosecution objected to this line of questioning and the objection was sustained. Judge Arird stated that that line of questioning was not going to be pursued.

Two more character witnesses testified for Mary: Fred Camp of Pittsfield and Steve Havanik of Torpedo. At 10:50 a.m. the defense rested.

Even though Mary was on trial for murder, reporters from newspapers across the state felt that their readers wanted to know all about the *femme fatale* that men were willing to kill for. Especially what she was wearing. One reporter wrote, "Mary wore a blue and white figured dress of sheer material, a shower bouquet of pink artificial flowers, and a dark felt hat with dark shoes and hose."

Once the reporter had captured Mary's appearance he turned to the courtroom that was overflowing with spectators. He wrote that many spectators brought their lunches right with them in the morning so that they wouldn't have to leave for the lunch recess and run the risk of losing their seats.

The reporter then interviewed a number of court spectators, many of whom were older residents, presumably able to come to the trial because they didn't have jobs to worry about. No one could remember a death penalty carried out in Warren County. One oldster recalled a local superstition that said that if a poor defendant were to be executed in Warren County, it would nullify the will of oil tycoon Henry R. Rouse. Rouse, they said, had left a fortune to the county to take care of the poor and to maintain county roads.

They told the reporter that the income from Rouse's legacy, which they claimed amounted to $10,000 a year, would revert to his heirs.

One version of the Rouse Legend (which is thought by many to be more myth than reality) has it that Rouse scrawled his will on the floor of an oil derrick building, which later exploded in 1861, burning Rouse to death. But after checking with local attorney William Glassman, the reporter assured the readers of his paper that no such clause was in the Rouse will.

Upon further investigation, however, it was learned that indeed there had been a death sentence handed down in Warren County. John Andrews was sentenced to death in 1912 for murder. But he appealed and the State Supreme Court ordered a new trial and a change of venue to Erie County. In the Erie trial Andrews was acquitted.

Interestingly, Andrews' attorney had been D. U. Arird, the very judge who was now trying the Mary Seminuk/Polens/Senauskas murder trials. In an aside to the reporter the Judge is quoted as saying, "Largest crowd in the courtroom since I defended Andrews twenty-four years ago."

CHAPTER VI

When the defense rested its case, Judge Arird began his instructions to the jury by saying, "Be governed only by evidence and not speeches of attorneys."

Arird continued, " Joe Senauskas is guilty of either first or second degree murder and that the jurors had to decide if Mary had any connection to the case."

At this point, Mary's attorney A. Lincoln Cohen stated that all proceedings of the trial be transcribed and preserved as part of the record in this case. It can be assumed that Cohen objected to the Judge's statement and, in case he would pursue an appeal, he wanted those statements preserved exactly as the judge had stated them.

Judge Arird noted Cohen's remarks then quoted the Act of 1860, which can make an "accessory before the fact" equally guilty with the principal in the case. Arird said that the jury could return one of three verdicts: not guilty, guilty of murder in the first degree or guilty of murder in the second degree. And, if they found Mary guilty of murder in the first degree, they must fix the penalty.

Judge Arird continued his instructions to the jury. He said that an Erie man had seen Polens and Mary in a beer garden in Erie and for that Metro could conceivably be angry with his wife. The Judge's remarks ran from 10 a.m. to 11:20 a.m., during which time Mary's attorney raised a number of objections only to have every one of them overruled.

Mary's mother, Mrs. Dora Zurkan, who had been held in the Warren jail as a material witness, was released the day before, on June 8,

31

at the conclusion of the testimony in Mary's trial. She did not testify

The newspaper reporter finished his article by telling his readers how Mary was holding up: "Mary appears thinner, her face is drawn; she looks as though she is suffering from nervous tension.

Mary's jury began deliberations at 11:25 a.m. on June 10. At 5:30 that afternoon, they had reached a verdict. The courtroom fell deadly silent as Mary was led to the defense table and the verdict was read. They had found Mary guilty of murder in the second degree.

Jury foreman H. V. Radspinner read the guilty verdict and stated the jury recommended that Mary serve up to twenty years.

In light of the events that would happen over the next few days when Arird himself would set Mary's sentence, the judge stated, "The jury must have felt sorry for her; but they did not disgrace themselves or other jurors of Warren County." He added, "Mary has had a hard life, always subjected to the rough side of things."

Still not finished, Arird pronounced, "John Polens is the cause of this." He added that Polens had confessed to paying Joe Senauskas to kill Mary's husband and that Polens had dominated Mary's life. Then Arird made the following remark to the packed courtroom: "May God forgive him. I can't."

On June 13, Judge Arird sentenced Mary to one-and-one-half to five years to be served at the Muncy Home for Women, plus a $100 fine and court costs. Mary was wearing the same beige dress she wore on June 3, the first day of her trial. She was permitted to remain seated while the sentence was read. The reporters noted that when the verdict was read Mary appeared "unaffected."

After Mary's sentence was read, Judge Arird addressed Mary: "It was your attorney Mr. Cohen who had the jury reduce the verdict from first to second degree. [It's not clear what Judge Arird meant by this statement. At no time did Cohen speak to the jury regarding the sentence. The best explanation I can offer is that the Judge simply misspoke. What he most likely meant to say was that Cohen had influenced *him* to reduce the jury's sentence. In light of what he said next, this explanation seems to make the most sense.]

"In the second place, he [Cohen] came to me privately and asked for a favor and I granted it. I honestly think I made a mistake. I intended to make the sentence from three to ten years. Maybe Mr. Cohen caught me in an easy moment. I don't know. But I am cutting the sentence in half."

The Judge hesitated then finished his remarks to Mary: "There is no pleasure in passing this sentence. When you come out, face the other way."

Mary was then led back to her cell, the place she had been calling home since May 13·

To a small group remaining in the court the judge said, perhaps by way of explaining his decision: "If we make a mistake, better to make it on the side of mercy."

CHAPTER VII

Now things started to heat up for Senauskas and Polens. In a published interview, Judge Arird stated that Senauskas had confessed to him that morning and that that confession would be the principal factor he would use to determine whether Senauskas should be charged with first or second degree murder. He added that he would not render the Senauskas decision until after Polens had his hearing the next day.

At his hearing before Judge Arird, Senauskas threw the first monkey wrench into the trial. Arird said that while Senauskas had made a full confession, he said also that Senauskas claimed he didn't remember anything from the night of the murder.

"I remember driving to the Garland Inn to get marijuana from Polens and that we smoked the marijuana and drank about a pint and a half of whiskey. But I don't remember anything else about that night. The next thing I remember was waking up the next morning," Senauskas testified.

After Senauskas finished his testimony, the only other witnesses to testify were the officers from the State Police who had arrested him. They reported that Senauskas had offered no resistance and that he had cooperated with them.

Polens followed the Senauskas monkey wrench by tossing in one of his own. He stated at his hearing that he had paid Senauskas to merely "warn the victim." Adding yet another twist to the story, Polens' attorney, A. Lincoln Cohen, announced that his client was a drug addict and not mentally stable.

Judge Arird agreed to a mental examination of Polens adding that he wanted a "yes or no answer" by the next Tuesday and if the answer from the exam turned out to be yes, that Polens was mentally ill, Arird would name a psychiatrist at that time.

At the hearing Polens' attorney A. Lincoln Cohen, also Mary's attorney, said, "Based on an Act of 1933, Polens could be classified as mentally and physically ill, as well as a drug addict. And therefore, it was correct that the judge defer sentencing until after Polens had been examined by a physician."

Although he claimed to be mentally ill, Polens was well enough to remember that Metro Seminuk had threatened to kill him four or five times. He said that his current mental condition started because of this strain and that he "was nervous all the time." He added that he became "jumpy" thinking he was going to be killed.

Polens continued, seemingly trying to shift the blame onto Metro Seminuk. He said he was not re-elected justice of the peace in Garland because he knew too much about Metro's alleged criminal affairs. He stated that Metro feared that he, Polens, would tell the authorities and Metro would be sent back to Canada, where he had entered the country.

Polens said that Metro told him that he had burned two airplane hangars on his property for the insurance money. He said Metro needed the money because he was delinquent on his gasoline taxes to the state Revenue Department. Polens ended his litany of Metro's wrongdoings by stating that when Metro took his trips to Erie he was smuggling aliens into this country from Canada.

Incredibly, after Polens had attempted to shift the blame onto the victim, he tried to shift the blame onto Senauskas. Polens said that after he had shared about his problems with Metro, Senauskas asked, "Why don't you have him taken care of?" To that Polens said he responded, "It all depends how you mean that."

This, Polens continued, led the pair to Cleveland where they met "a guy" at a Greek restaurant to discuss the Metro problem. After they left the restaurant Polens said that Senauskas told him "It was all taken care of."

When nothing came of this conversation, Polens said that Senauskas told him, "If he [Metro] doesn't promise to be good, I'll take care of him in my own way." Polens admitted that he knew at that point that Senauskas meant to kill Metro.

Even as far along as the day before the murder and up to the point where they had already rented the getaway car, Polens contended that he tried to stop Senauskas from going through with the murder. Polens stated that he said to Senauskas, "We should take the car back and forget all about it." To this, Polens testified that Senauskas responded, "We've gone this far, we might as well go through with it."

Polens continued, telling the court that Senauskas told him that he and his girlfriend had pulled an $18,000 job [a burglary] in Munhall near Pittsburgh, but there was a fire in the hotel in which they were staying and the money went up in smoke. Polens said this ought to show the court how desperate Senauskas was for money.

After attempting to set the blame on Metro and or Senauskas, Polens told about himself. He said he was a dope addict and that he took opium in a pill form. He began his habit in 1929 when he drove taxi in Pittsburgh and by the time he was having his talks with Senauskas, his mind was "not normal." Polens admitted that he'd had dope smuggled into his cell at the Warren County Jail and that when his supply ran out, he got sick and had to be treated by a physician.

Polens testified that he had graduated from Duquesne University with a bachelor's degree in economics in 1927. He then started law school but had to drop out because he was "on the verge of a nervous breakdown." It was then, he continued, that his physician advised him to get out in the open and in 1929 his family purchased the farm they still owned in Garland.

When asked about the murder weapon, Polens admitted that he had given the .38 caliber handgun to Senauskas because Senauskas said he was a marked man and that he was afraid he would be killed by gangsters. This ended Polens' testimony.

June Bryce and Mae Clancy testified next. They said Polens was of good character and that he visited them often. [This appears to be an attempt on Cohen's part to show that Polens couldn't have been having an affair with Mary Seminuk because he was in fact busy courting these two women.] The next witness, Warren attorney Harold Hampson, testified to Polens' good character.

After the conclusion of Polens' hearing Judge Arird reiterated that he would take no action on Senauskas' case until after Polens' psychiatric examination next Tuesday.

On Monday, June 15 Judge Arird announced to the press that

arguments for the degree of murder phase in the trials of Senauskas and Polens would be heard the next Friday. He said that Polens had been evaluated at the Warren State Hospital during a session that lasted from 10 A.M. until 4 P.M. and that the results of that evaluation would be made known on Friday.

In that same newspaper article it was reported that Warren County Jail Matron Mrs. Ernest Berdine and her husband, Warden Berdine had the preceding Saturday driven Mary to the Muncy Home for Women, which is just east of Williamsport. They left Warren at one o'clock—for the 209-mile trip—and arrived in Muncy at 6:45 P.M. Mrs. Berdine reported that Mary had "cried and screamed, and fainted three times during the trip and when we arrived she broke down completely and was placed in the hospital at Muncy."

On Friday, June 19 a number of significant irregularities in the Senauskas-Polens murder trials occurred in Judge Arird's courtroom. First, Judge Arird referred to the light sentence of one-and-one-half to five years he had handed down on Mary. He stated that "it costs taxpayers four dollars a week to board inmates and that the taxpayers should be considered in passing sentence."

Arird stated that murder in the first degree is punishable by death or life in prison while murder in the second degree carries a maximum punishment of twenty years in prison.

The second problem that day was that Senauskas' attorney, Earle V. MacDonald, was ill and unable to attend the proceedings. Never-the-less, District Attorney L.C. Eddy presented his case for the prosecution, namely that because the murder was premeditated it was indeed a murder in the first degree. He concluded that while it may be true that Polens had the symptoms of an "opium eater," there was no indication that the confessed murderer was insane.

Polens' attorney, A. Lincoln Cohen, argued against Eddy's statements. Then he pointed out that Polens was the son of poor Polish immigrants who had settled in the "strip" district in Pittsburgh. Cohen said also "there are definite traces of insanity on the mother's side of the family."

Cohen pointed out that, despite his background, his client had tried to elevate himself by finishing high school and going to college. But as a result of having had scarlet fever, Polens was left with a nervous condition. And this condition accounted for the frustrations his client had experienced in life. He added that these failures and frustrations climaxed with the murder of Metro Seminuk.

Then, incredibly, Cohen ended his remarks with the following statement: "As to Polens' moral background, the less said the better."

In what would prove to be a truly bizarre day in Warren County jurisprudence, Judge Arird put the capper on the day. Instead of postponing the hearing until MacDonald was able to attend and to defend his client on a murder charge, he would extend him the courtesy of making his argument in person or in writing the following Monday.

Although MacDonald's health—and his untimely death—would become a major factor in Senauskas' trial, Monday morning the attorney was in court, arguing his case in front of Judge Arird. His first statement was that when he advised Senauskas to plead guilty, he believed his client was pleading guilty to murder in the second degree.

His point was that he as an attorney would never advise a client to plead guilty to murder in the first degree because of the unmitigated severity of the punishment. To carry it one step further, Who would plead guilty to the worst possible outcome—life in prison or death in the electric chair? The defendant would be better off to go to trial where he at least would have a chance of being convicted of murder in the second degree. No. It was his belief that when a defendant pleaded guilty to murder in the Commonwealth of Pennsylvania in 1936, it should be understood and goes without saying that he is pleading guilty to murder in the second degree.

Then MacDonald made a dramatic statement: "It is the duty of the Commonwealth in its desire to raise the degree of murder to first degree to prove by facts beyond a reasonable doubt that all elements of a murder in the first degree exist. I believe, as a representative of Joe Senauskas and the Court, the Commonwealth has failed."

MacDonald continued, saying that in order to prove murder in the first degree, the prosecution had to prove there was specific intent. And that nothing in Senauskas' signed confession gave any inkling that the defendant knew what he was doing from 9:30 on the night of March 26 until he awoke Friday morning, March 27 at 9 A.M. Therefore, he had no intent. Because of the marijuana and liquor Senauskas used that day, he couldn't realize what he was doing.

MacDonald said that Senauskas was raised without a mother and that this was a major factor in how Senauskas turned out in life. He said that when Senauskas shared his troubles with his girlfriend Katherine

Kowalski—especially his most current problem in Cleveland—that Katherine told Polens about him and that he smoked marijuana and that it would be easy to put pressure on him to get him to cooperate in the murder.

MacDonald took yet another tack. He argued that because Mary had been convicted of murder in the second degree, it would be inconsistent for the court to ask for murder in the first degree for his client. Plus, he added Senauskas had sent money to a lawyer in Cleveland to take care of another matter; he wanted to return to Cleveland and get himself clear.

MacDonald's final statement was that Senauskas should be sent to prison. He should be punished so that he could come out of prison and start a new life.

When it was his turn, District Attorney Eddy jumped up and countered MacDonald's argument: "If Senauskas and Polens are guilty of premeditated murder, then they are guilty of murder in the first degree. Senauskas knew what he was doing when he took the money from Polens. That money was nothing but blood money."

District Attorney Eddy ended by saying, "This is as cold-blooded a murder as ever committed in Warren County."

Judge Arird ended the proceedings that day with the following explanation of what is meant by *intent* in a murder case. "After an intention is formed to kill, the killing is not founded on the intent, but the intent is founded on the killing."

On the morning of Tuesday, June 23, 1936 Warren County President Judge D. U. Arird walked into Courtroom One of the Warren County Courthouse and called the sentencing of Joe Senauskas to order. He directed that the defendant, Joe Senauskas, alias Joe Sennette, alias Gerald Chapman, stand while he made his opening remarks.

"You have left the court with an unpleasant duty. You have no defense. You are convicted by your plea, by your confession and by the testimony presented of the murder in the first degree."

Asked if he had anything to say, Senauskas held his gaze to the floor and responded in a low, almost inaudible, voice: "I had no intention to kill and I don't remember anything that happened."

Judge Arird then read the following: "And now, June 23, 1936, the sentence of the law is that you, Joe Senauskas, alias Joe Sennette, alias, Gerald Chapman be taken hence by the Sheriff of Warren County to the jail of that county from whence you came, and from thence in due course to the Western Penitentiary[1] in Centre County, Pennsylvania, and that you suffer death during the week fixed by the Governor of the Commonwealth, in a building erected for that purpose on land owned by the Commonwealth, such punishment being inflicted by the warden or deputy warden of Western Penitentiary, or by such person as the warden shall designate, by causing to pass through your body a current of electricity of intensity sufficient to cause death and the application of such current to be continued until you are dead. May God in his infinite goodness, have mercy on your soul."

Senauskas stood dazed and wiped his forehead with his handkerchief. He was plainly shocked and surprised by the severity of the punishment.

The courtroom fell silent as Sheriff Berdine took Senauskas by the arm to support him and began to lead him out of the courtroom. The silence was broken when Senauskas shook his arm free and said, "I'm all right."

Immediately after Senauskas was escorted out his attorney Earle MacDonald took exception to the finding of the court and asked that all testimony in the case be transcribed and those records be certified by the court prothonotary. Judge Arird granted the request.

***

John Polens was then led into the courtroom and as soon as he was seated at the defense table, Judge Arird informed him that his attorney A. Lincoln Cohen had sent a telegram to the court. It stated that he couldn't be present today and he didn't know when he would be able to return to Warren. Judge Arird said that he wasn't going to delay Polens' sentencing. Then he added, "He's done all he can for you."

Judge Arird followed the same procedure that he had with Senauskas then he asked Polens if he had anything to say. Polens responded, "I think it was explained to us at first that clemency would be given if we pleaded guilty. I myself don't think I was mentally able to take care of myself at the time. If I had, I wouldn't have done this. I ask the court for clemency."

Judge Arird responded, "If there were any extenuating circumstances in this case, I don't recall it. I don't recall any favorable circumstances. It was deliberated, premeditated, plotted and planned to kill a human being. There is nothing to do but find you guilty and pronounce sentence."

Judge Arird then read the same death sentence he had read to Senauskas.

To anyone who had been in the courtroom throughout the case it was becoming clear that it was not enough for Judge Arird to administer justice. He had to add a reprimand to these defendants and or offer an explanation to those in the courtroom.

In Mary's case it appeared that he felt the need to explain why he had pronounced such a light sentence. His follow up statement in her case was that because it costs taxpayers $4 a day to board a prisoner, he took the taxpayers' interest in mind when he sentenced her to only one-and-one-half to five years.

Then, as if there were *anything* a judge could say to someone after he has just pronounced a death sentence on him, Judge Arird found it necessary to add a codicil to his sentencing of Senauskas. His after-sentencing remark to Senauskas was: "It has developed in this case that you have a considerable knowledge of crimes and criminals."

After he sentenced Polens to death he added: "Polens, I'm going to repeat. It isn't a pleasant duty. It's hard. But the law leaves nothing else to do."

As with Senauskas, Polens then was removed from the courtroom and escorted to his cell in the Warren County Jail.

CHAPTER VIII

Before the ink was dry on Senauskas' and Polens' death sentences their lawyers began an appeal to the Supreme Court of Pennsylvania. While much of the language of the affidavits of appeal is written in the necessary legalistic style of the day, the core of their appeals was "an injustice was done in sentencing the men to the electric chair."

If an appeal were to be granted, the court would have two options. It could change the first-degree murder charge to second-degree murder, in which case the court would set a new sentence. The sentence would have to be something other than the death penalty since the death penalty applies only to first degree murder. Or the court could stay with the first-degree murder charge and it could change the sentence from death to life in prison. If their appeals were denied, the condemned men could then take their case to the governor of Pennsylvania, at this time George Howard Earle. Or they could go before the state board of pardons to ask for a commutation of the sentence, in which case the men would be sentenced to life in prison.

In the meantime, the borough of Warren learned firsthand that the wheels of justice turn slowly and sometimes those same wheels run right over the men and institutions who are trying to speed things along. In the case of Senauskas and Polens, no sooner had the sheriffs begun preparing the prisoners for their trip to Death Row in Rockview Prison, when they were informed that prisoners who were condemned to die were held in the jail of the county where they were sentenced until three days prior to their execution date. In other words, the prisoners would be staying in the

Warren County Jail until all their appeals were exhausted.

***

In England in 1487 the Star Chamber was established in the British courts. The Star Chamber was a set of rules, laws, and regulations that authorized authorities to torture defendants in order to get a confession. It also required defendants to sign an oath to answer all questions asked of them, including those that might demonstrate guilt. But as England and the rest of Europe moved forward from the Dark Ages, this barbaric practice was left behind and in 1641 the Parliament abolished the Star Chamber. At this point a right was written into English common law that protected defendants from self-incrimination.

In 1676 the Duke of York imposed the British code of law on the American colonies. After the colonies won the Revolutionary War and gained their freedom from England, the new laws they set forth were based on English common law. In doing this they included the provision that a defendant could not be forced to witness against himself; this provision was included in the Bill of Rights and is known as the Fifth Amendment.

Despite the fact that the Fifth Amendment was on the books, many police departments continued to use force, threats, and false promises to get defendants to confess. Studies showed that these tactics were used routinely—even into the 1930s. From that point forward these same studies also showed that physical force and brutality were being phased out by a new form of persuasion: psychological coercion. This included keeping prisoners isolated, lying to them about evidence against them, and participating in marathon questioning sessions.

All this changed however in 1966 when the Supreme Court overturned the 1963 rape and kidnapping conviction of a twenty-three-year-old Arizona truck driver named Ernesto Miranda. After police arrested Miranda they questioned him for two hours, at the end of which he confessed. On appeal, Miranda's lawyers argued that this period of questioning was at its least intimidating and that this intimidation had compelled Miranda to confess. Writing for the five to four majority Chief Justice Earl Warren wrote that in an intimidating environment, in which police questioning takes place, there is a strong potential for forced confessions.

As a result of this ruling, which was based on a number of similar appeals as well, the Court came up with the following guidelines: Before a suspect is questioned by police, they must warn him that (1) he has the right to remain silent (2) any statements he makes can be used against him (3) he has the right to have an attorney present (4) if he can't afford an attorney, one will be appointed (without charge to the defendant).

Of course none of these guidelines were in place in 1936 during the investigation and subsequent murder trials of John Polens and Joseph Senauskas. But these guidelines and other germane points of law were on the mind of one attorney during America's very own Dark Ages in criminal justice. Although Earle V. MacDonald was court appointed, he was by no means a second-rate attorney. His appeal before the state Supreme Court for Senauskas listed no less than twenty-three places in the record where he felt his client did not receive due process of law.

MacDonald's position, simply put, was that even if Senauskas pleaded guilty, and even if he *were* guilty, he was not treated fairly. His first point was that the Court erred in not fixing the degree of the crime prior to the sentence of the defendant. His point begs the question: Who would plead guilty to murder if he knew—*in advance*—that he would receive the death penalty?

It's important to remember that both Senauskas and Polens forsook a trial by jury, opting instead for a bench trial, which is a trial presided over by one judge. And, they pleaded guilty before Judge Arird. On the first day of the hearing, June 2, Senauskas pleaded not guilty, then when the first jurors were being chosen the next morning, June 3, he abruptly changed his plea to guilty. It will never be known what—if anything—was said between Senauskas and MacDonald that morning. It will never be known why Senauskas changed his plea. Did MacDonald advise his client to plead guilty to show the court he was cooperating and was saving everyone's time—and the taxpayers' money? After all, there was no disputing his guilt. Did MacDonald already have a deal in place with Judge Arird? Or did he think he could work out a deal with the judge, perhaps appeal to the judge that his client was still a teenager?

There were conflicting reports regarding this crucial turn of events. Did MacDonald have a deal or didn't he? It's easy to picture these two officers of the court slipping into the judge's chambers and discussing the case. But then what?

If you look at Judge Delford U. Arird's portrait hanging above the second floor landing of the steps in the Warren County Courthouse, you see a man who appears secure in the decisions he's made for his life.

Although he had never married and never had children, the word paternalistic comes to mind. Based on the success of his life and career, one could say that throughout his life he made all the right moves. Here was a man who was used to being in charge, a no-nonsense, salt-of-the-earth farmer's son who had risen in rank and community standard far beyond his upbringing.

In his portrait, wisps of fluffy white hair lay across his balding head, and like other men his age, remnants of his gray-white hair encircle his pate. He's wearing a dark, three-piece suit with a high-collar white shirt, and although you can't see it, it's easy to assume that in his left vest pocket there is a watch, connected to a fob, whose end is secure in his right vest pocket. On Sunday, May 31, 1936—just three days prior to the fateful June 2 courtroom fiasco—Judge Delford U. Arird celebrated his eighty-fifth birthday.

***

Attorney Earle Vincent MacDonald was born August 10, 1878, graduated from Allegheny College, and was admitted to the bar in June 1903. He had been in practice in the city of Warren ever since. At fifty-seven, MacDonald was twenty-eight years younger than Arird and his manner of dress spoke of a man who dressed for his times. He wore his hair parted on the side and used a hair tonic to keep it in place; and had a penchant to wear bow ties with a white shirt.

MacDonald was a "preacher's son." His father was the highly regarded Rev. John Calvin MacDonald. Aside from being an attorney, MacDonald was a principal in a number of businesses in Warren, including the Barnhart-Davis Machine Shop. He had been president of the Conewango Valley Country Club and had been the Exalted Ruler and a District Deputy of the Warren Lodge of the Elks, a member of the Scottish Rites and the Masons.

In short, MacDonald did not seem to be the type of man that would fabricate a story—for any reason, whether in his law practice or in his personal or fraternal life. Why would he make up a story? Why would a successful lawyer and businessman, a father of three children, jeopardize his reputation for a confessed killer?

There are two possible answers to these questions, and they're both based on a physical rather than a moral or legal issue. Judge Arird was eighty-five-years-old: was his memory fading? At fifty-seven, MacDonald was in the prime of his life and career—or was he? He had been ill and had missed some court sessions while covering this case. In the vernacular of that day, he was reported to have a "brain ailment." Did this ailment affect his memory?

Did MacDonald and Arird have a deal and did Arird actually *forget* they had made a deal? Or did Judge Arird *intimate in some way* that if the defendant pleaded guilty he would hand down a lesser sentence? Did MacDonald not hear him correctly or did he misinterpret something the judge said?

There was nothing in writing—or better stated there was never anything in writing produced on June 3. When speaking to others about this day MacDonald insisted there was a deal in place and that Arird had simply forgotten the conversation. (Key evidence would surface a few months later that would shed new light on the June 3 meeting between Judge Arird and attorney MacDonald.)

MacDonald's second point was that nothing regarding the first point was ever put in writing, so that his client could look it over and if necessary reject the language.

His third point was that even though his client pleaded guilty to murder, he did not plead guilty to the *willful, deliberate, and premeditated killing* of Metro Seminuk. MacDonald's reasoning here was that while his client pleaded guilty to murder, he did not admit to those three words, which needed to be in place to prove first degree murder.

Point four was that since Senauskas had his trial before Polens, the fact that Polens confessed to his part in the slaying added to the premeditated aspect of the murder, which was not in evidence at Senauskas' trial. In other words, Senauskas pleaded guilty, then Polens pleaded guilty and inherent in Polen's confession was the fact that there was a plan to kill Metro Seminuk. But, since Polens' confession was not in place at the time of Senauskas' trial—it was not in evidence—the evidence put forth by Polens should not be admissible in any consideration of Senauskas' case.

Point five asserted that the Court talked with State Police investigators and members of the sheriff's department about Senauskas's mental and physical condition without the defendant or his lawyer present.

Point six stated that the court drew conclusions based on the confession of John Polens, which was not an item in Senauskas' case. While point six seems to be a reiteration of the fourth point, it's not. Point four objects to the fact that the court, in effect, connected Senauskas' and

Polens confessions. Point six, however, concerns itself with the language of Polens' confession: that certain things he said were used as evidence against Senauskas. Point four objects to what was done and point six objects to what specifically was said. For example, when Polens said that he and Senauskas drove to Buffalo to rent a car, this statement was used against Senauskas to prove a plan to kill was in place and that it was willful and premeditated. MacDonald was saying that this statement couldn't be used against Senauskas because it was not in evidence at Senauskas' trial.

In point seven MacDonald objected to the fact that statements Senauskas made to police officers and in the presence of the warden regarding his life in crime and the criminals he knew were used against Senauskas in his trial. The point is here that apparently Senauskas told the deputies that he had led a life a crime—perhaps he even boasted about his crimes and underworld connections—and the deputies conveyed these statements to the judge and they were used against Senauskas.

MacDonald was saying that regardless of what his client may have said, whether it was true or not, it was not in evidence at Senauskas' trial. For example, let's say Senauskas boasted to police about knowing a hit man in Cleveland, before that statement could be used in court, the prosecution would have to produce its own evidence to the court to support this in order to use this evidence against Senauskas. The prosecution would have had to take each statement that it wanted to use and substantiate it via corroborating evidence that it was true. Clearly, this was not done.

Point eight concerned the fact that police stated at trial that the defendant, at the time of his arrest, seemed "natural and perfectly normal." MacDonald asserted that these facts were not in evidence at Senauskas' trial. Here again, MacDonald was saying there is no proof to back up these claims.

Point nine attacked the fact that before Judge Arird made the following statement he conferred with the warden of the Warren County Jail and other police personnel. "Consequently we find no mitigating circumstances and no extenuating circumstances and taking into consideration all the surrounding circumstances there is nothing to move the conscience of the court to delay these proceedings."

Short and sweet: MacDonald was asserting that Judge Arird had had talks with law enforcement personnel to get a feel for what kind of person the defendant was. And he did this without the defendant or his lawyer in the room—a clear violation of fundamental law in that a defendant has the right to confront his accusers. Senauskas was not present at these talks and therefore, MacDonald stated anything that was said in these talks is inadmissible in court.

Points ten, eleven, and twelve again objected to the two confessions being linked together. We can assume that since this issue has been put forth in a number of objections, that in each instance MacDonald is objecting to a separate aspect of the confession. One point may cover the statement by Polens that they rented the car, another that he gave Senauskas the gun, another that they took target practice.

Point thirteen stated that the Court erred when it put forth the following statement made by Judge Arird: "It is clearly proven and in fact, virtually admitted that Joe Senauskas intended to take the life of Metro Seminuk. Deliberation and premeditation as required by the State are not upon the intent, but upon the killing. It is deliberation and premeditation enough to form the intent to kill and not upon the intent after it has been formed. The intent distinctly formed even 'for a moment' before it is carried into act, is enough, and while waiting for Tom Bower to leave, Joe Senauskas had ample time to deliberate and premeditate enough to form the intent to kill."

Point fourteen asserted that the Court erred in the following finding of fact: "When Joe Senauskas entered a plea of guilty he admitted that he was guilty of willful, deliberate and premeditated killing of Metro Seminuk as no other kind of murder was charged in the indictment. Now for him to attempt to show that he did not realize what he was doing at the time he shot to death Metro Seminuk would be manifestly inconsistent with his plea of guilty."

Point fifteen asserted that the Court erred in the following finding of fact: "John G. Polens and Joe Senauskas admitted that John G. Polens was an accessory before the fact" that same being passed upon admissions of John G. Polens which was not in evidence in this case.

Point sixteen asserted that the Court erred in the following finding of fact, the same being based upon the confession of Polens and Polens' admissions, which were not in evidence in this case.

Point seventeen asserted that the Court erred in the following finding of fact: "John G. Polens and Joe Senauskas not only deliberated and premeditated together, but they planned just when, where and how the killing of Metro Seminuk should be done" which said finding of fact is based partially upon the confession of John G. Polens, which is not in evidence in this case.

Point eighteen asserted that the Court erred in the following finding of fact: "In the opinion of the State Police and the Deputy Sheriff that arrested these defendants, the defendants were natural and perfectly normal. The evidence fails to show from the time these defendants, in open court, entered pleas of guilty, down to the present time, that their minds are not normal" which facts were not in evidence in this case.

Point nineteen asserted that the Court erred in the following finding of fact: "Polens claims he was afraid of Seminuk because Seminuk had threatened him. That statement is inconsistent with the facts as Polens admitted he visited the home of Seminuk almost daily, and it was proven that when Seminuk was attending church, Polens would go to Seminuk's home and remain for a long period of time. Besides he took Mrs. Seminuk to the City of Erie a number of times and one of the witnesses testified that in a beer garden he drank beer with Polens and Mrs. Seminuk until one o'clock in the morning, and when Mrs. Seminuk was on the witness stand for herself, she did not even deny these facts," none of which facts appear as evidence in this case.

Point twenty asserted that the Court erred in its finding of murder of the degree as murder in the first degree in this case for the reason that it went without the record, and as is shown by its opinion, conversed with parties not under oath without having such conversations in the presence of the defendant or his counsel and basing his findings that there were no extenuating circumstances from conversations had with officers and others not upon the record.

Point twenty-one stated that the court erred in its statement, which is not part of its opinion or decree or sentence as filed in the above entitled case, when it stated to the defendant, after asking him if he had anything to say as to why sentence should not be pronounced, and being aware thereto the Court stated: "Let me say to you young man, that crimes are committed by young men all through the country, throughout the world, through the United States, and it has developed in this case, in my opinion, that you have considerable knowledge relating to crimes and criminals. The sentence I pronounce against you is the sentence provided by the Supreme Court", and thereupon the Court proceeded to read the sentence as appears in the written finding and sentence of the Court.

Point twenty-two stated that the Court erred in its sentence in that the said sentence, in accordance with said opinion, is based upon conversations not under oath had with persons, which are not of record in said case, and were had by the Court with said officers and persons not in the presence of the defendant or his counsel or with an opportunity by the defendant or his counsel to examine or cross-examine the said persons in order to ascertain the truth of said alleged statements.

Point twenty-three asserted that the defendant did not receive a fair and impartial trial as guaranteed by the Constitution of the Commonwealth for the reason that the opinion, findings and judgement of the court were influenced by talks with persons not under oath or subject to cross-examination, and by other matters dehors the record. [The word *dehors* is French for outside. In legal proceedings, it refers to that which is irrelevant or outside the scope of the debate.] The motion then ended:

"WHEREFORE, the said defendant prays that the judgement and sentence be arrested in this case and that a new trial be granted.

The defendant, by his attorney, further moves for leave to file additional exceptions, if necessary, after the testimony has been transcribed and certified.

Attorney for Defendant"

***

According to his attorney, Earle MacDonald, Joe Senauskas got the shaft. But consider the case of John Polens: his attorney A. Lincoln Cohen didn't even show up for his client's sentencing. Instead, according to the statement Polens made just before his sentencing, Cohen told him to plead guilty and that a deal had been made wherein he would not get the electric chair. At this point it must be assumed that Cohen and MacDonald had conferred outside the courtroom sometime prior to the sentencing date and it appears that MacDonald informed Cohen that such a deal was also in place for Polens if he pleaded guilty.

Cohen must have thought that it was a done deal for his client as well. He didn't even bother to attend. We must assume that he thought the deal would go through and the defendants would be sentenced to life in prison. His thinking at the time may have been that his client would go to Western Penitentiary, keep his nose clean and, hopefully, someday get out on parole. For a confessed murderer, what more could a defendant wish for? Plus, through some kind of skullduggery with Judge Arird (that was alluded to by Judge Arird at Mary's sentencing but never explained), he was able to get his second client, Mary Seminuk, off with the proverbial slap on the wrist.

Not bad for someone arguing two cases at the same time, and over 100 miles from his office to boot. But of course all those plans went out the window when Judge Arird sentenced Polens to death. But still, even the most naïve observer must have asked himself how could two defendants, Mary and Polens, both commit the same crime: accessory to murder before the fact, and one get one-and-one-half to five years and the other get the death penalty? Was it because Mary was a beautiful, young woman and Polens was a fallen justice of the peace, a disgrace to the legal community?

Two days after MacDonald filed his appeal, Cohen filed an appeal for Polens at the Supreme Court in Pittsburgh, as follows: "My brief contends the guilty plea was coerced. We ask to withdraw the guilty plea, entered on advice of counsel that the judge agreed to leniency and said he [Polens] would not be electrocuted."

That same day, June 29, the Supreme Court in Philadelphia had already granted a rule to show cause on the motion by Attorney Earle MacDonald for a stay of execution and a new trial for Joe Senauskas. Warren Prothonotary J.V. Blair confirmed that his office had received a copy of the ruling from the Supreme Court.

Within days of filing his appeal Cohen received an answer from Justice James B. Drew. Drew issued a stay order and in the same filing directed Judge Arird to show cause why the petitions should not be granted. In other words, after reading the appeals by MacDonald and Cohen, justices of the Supreme Court felt that there was enough of a discrepancy to warrant looking into the matter and that Judge Arird and District Attorney L.C. Eddy should prepare their side of the argument. Both cases were scheduled to be heard during the September session.

CHAPTER IX

While it appeared that MacDonald's Supreme Court appeal was receiving serious consideration, another aspect of the attorney's life was moving in the opposite direction. On August 10, MacDonald celebrated his fifty-eighth birthday, but a little over two weeks after that, on August 28, he died from complications as a result of emergency brain surgery performed in Philadelphia.

By September 22, 1936 Warren County Judge Delford U. Arird and District Attorney L.C. Eddy had prepared their response to the affidavits of appeals filed by the lawyers for Warren County's most notorious guests: nineteen-year-old Joe Senauskas and thirty-one-year-old John Polens, who had celebrated his thirty-first birthday on June 25. The men spent the summer in the Warren County Jail under 24-hour security provided by the Sheriff's Department.

On September 23, Eddy transported the necessary papers to the State Supreme Court in Philadelphia, where the Senauskas appeal was filed. Those papers consisted of copies of testimony, docket entries, opinions, and all other records of the cases of Senauskas and Polens. Although the appeal of each defendant would be heard and ruled upon separately, the casework for both trials was delivered at this time. Originally, Polens' appeal was filed by his attorney A. L. Cohen in the Pittsburgh branch of the State Supreme Court.

The justices of the Supreme Court informed local authorities that it would hear no more argument or evidence in the cases. They stated they would review the cases and decide upon a further course of action. They had a number of options. They could dismiss the appeals, grant a hearing and further argument, refer the matter to another court for a retrial, or they could change the death penalty sentences to life imprisonment sentences.

On September 23, the State Supreme Court in Philadelphia announced that the hearing for convicted killer Joe Senauskas would be held the following Monday, September 28. On October 1, word had reached Warren officials that the court had ruled in favor of the prisoners' request. The Court was sending Judge James I. Brownson of Washington County and President Judge of the 27th Judicial District to proceed forthwith to Warren and hear the motions, not only for an amended plea, but also for new trials and the arrest of the death sentence delivered by Judge Arird.

The court instructed also that Judge Brownson investigate the complaint of the defendants that they had changed their pleas to guilty under an "agreement or understanding" that if found guilty of murder in the first degree they would not receive the death penalty. Judge Brownson was given full powers to ascertain the facts, call witnesses, and appoint attorneys; he was instructed to make a full report with recommendations.

When confronted with this latest development by reporters, Judge Arird responded, "I have no criticism to offer. I do not know Judge Brownson, but I believe him to be an able man." The judge then added something new to the mix: "Neither Cohen nor the late Earle MacDonald in their arguments as to degree and sentence mentioned any representation of leniency as was charged in their appeals to the Supreme Court."

In other words, when both lawyers filed their affidavits of appeal, they asked for a lot of things but neither specifically asked Judge Arird for leniency.

District Attorney L.C. Eddy said, "I believe that by sending an outside judge to Warren, the Supreme Court is attempting to give full and careful consideration to both sides in this case. And once the facts are known, I'm confident the local court ruling will be upheld."

One of the supreme ironies of this case was the selection of President Judge James I. Brownson to hold the upcoming hearing. Brownson, who was born January 25, 1856, was eighty years old. In its infinite wisdom, the Supreme Court had sent an *eighty-year-old-man to verify the memory of an eighty-five-year-old man.* In fact, before Brownson was finished with the case, he would be over eighty-one *years of age.*

When hearing of the Supreme Court's decision to send the Washington County judge to Warren to get to the bottom of things, Judge Arird said he didn't know Brownson, but thought he was an able man. Arird didn't have to know Brownson; their lives and careers were so similar, they could have been brothers or classmates. Both men were from highly regarded families where words like integrity, hard work, and honesty were most likely the watchwords in family discussions. One major difference, however, was that while Arird came from a farming family, Brownson came from an illustrious family in which he could trace his roots back to the Revolutionary War.

Judge Brownson's father was the Reverend James I. Brownson. The elder Brownson graduated from Washington College and the Western Theological Seminary in Pittsburgh. He was a distinguished Presbyterian minister for fifty years. Rev. Brownson's father James Brownson was a major in the War of 1812 and the major's father, Dr. Richard Brownson, was a surgeon in the Revolutionary War.

Judge James I. Brownson graduated from Washington and Jefferson College in 1875 at age nineteen. He passed the bar in 1878 and went into private practice until he was appointed judge in the Court of Common Pleas in Washington County in 1918. The next year he was elected to that post for a ten-year term and in 1929 he was again elected to serve another ten-year term. In 1922 he was appointed president judge of Washington County Courts, the position he held when he was chosen by the Supreme Court to hold the Senauskas-Polens hearing.

***

Unlike the early days of the murder trials of Mary Seminuk, Senauskas, and Polens, when every seat in the courtroom was taken, when Judge Brownson opened the court on the morning of October 6, very few spectators were present. Polens' attorney A.L. Cohen sent word that he would be unable to attend the proceedings. There were two new faces, however. One was local attorney Harold Hampson, who was appointed by Judge Brownson to represent Senauskas during this trial. The Judge pointed out that Hampson would represent Senauskas in this trial only.

***

Harold S. Hampson was born in Warren on October 6, 1897. He graduated from Warren High School in 1915 and studied secretarial skills at Hoff Business College in Warren and then entered the U.S. Army and was appointed a warrant officer. He served in France, Germany, and Belgium as secretary to General John Pershing, Commander-in-Chief of the American Expeditionary Forces in Europe during World War I. Hamspon accompanied General Pershing on their return to America aboard the steamship "Leviathan", arriving in America on September 8, 1919.

Hampson then attended Wharton School of Finance and Commerce of the University of Pennsylvania and graduated in 1922. He next entered University of Michigan Law School and graduated in 1929. He was admitted to the Warren County Bar Association in 1929 and began practicing law with his father Thomas Lee Hamspon, also an attorney.

The thirty-nine-year-old Hampson had been practicing law seven years when he was appointed Joe Senauskas' attorney by Judge Arird.

The second new face in the courtroom that fall morning was Philadelphia attorney L. B. Schofield, who had been retained by Judge Arird to represent him.

Judge Brownson then gave his instructions as to what would be taking place. He set Tuesday, October 27 as the date for the trial to begin and instructed Prothonotary J.V. Blair to subpoena the witnesses. He noted that testimony for both cases would be heard on the same day.

A week and a day later, on Wednesday, October 14, one of the principal investigators in the Seminuk murder case made a surprise visit to Warren. Private John Mehallick of the Pennsylvania State Police was a main player in the investigation and had testified in the subsequent murder trials of the three defendants. Mehallick, who had since been transferred to the Butler State Police Barracks, was stationed at the Kane barracks at the time of the murder.

Although Mehallick did disclose to the press that he had returned to Warren County two weeks before the other witnesses in the case with the express intent of doing further investigation, he did not disclose what the nature or the scope of his investigation would be.

"All I can say at this time," the officer stated, "is that my investigation will have a direct bearing on the upcoming hearings."

CHAPTER X

When visiting Judge James I. Brownson opened the hearings regarding the appeals of convicted killers Joe Senauskas and John Polens in the Warren County Courthouse on Tuesday morning, October 27, 1936, a number of new players had been added to the cast of characters. However, before any witnesses were called Senauskas' newly appointed attorney Harold Hampson and Polens' attorney A.L.Cohen challenged the legality of having Philadelphia Assistant District Attorney Lemuel B. Schofield represent Judge Arird and the Commonwealth. They cited a rule of court that stated in such a case, as was before them, a local attorney must be used. Their objection was denied.

The first new player was Miss Ethel B. Baldensperger, secretary for the late Earle V. MacDonald. If you searched central casting you couldn't find a more appropriate actress to play Attorney MacDonald's secretary than Miss Baldensperger. At the time of the trial, Miss Baldensperger was forty-three-years-old and unmarried. In fact, she would remain a "Miss" until her death on November 22, 1967. The truth of the matter was that on that October morning in 1936, Miss Baldensperger was still mourning the unexpected death of her employer and the effect his death had had on her life.

In 1948 she would take the position of Warren County tax collector and she would remain there until her retirement from that post in 1958. She was active in her church, the Grace Methodist and was a member of a number of Christian organizations, such as the Truth Seekers Class, the Women's Society of Christian Service, and the Virginia Miller

Circle at her church.

In short, no one in the courtroom that day who knew Miss Baldensperger would have any reason to question her veracity. It was inconceivable that she would tell a lie. She was, as the saying goes, a pillar of the community. Yet, here she was in the middle of a mystery that centered on an *ex parte* affidavit filed by her boss, Earle V. MacDonald on June 25, 1936.

Ex parte is a Latin term meaning "for one party only." Legally speaking, it refers to those proceedings where one of the parties has not received notice, and therefore, is neither present nor represented. The *ex parte* proceedings that interested the court that morning was the affidavit Earle MacDonald made on June 25, 1936 and subsequently filed with the State Supreme Court.

This raises a few questions: Why did MacDonald file such a document? He had been ill before his death and even had to cut short a trip he had made to Western United States, where he attended the Shrine convention in Seattle and the annual Elk convention in Los Angeles. And, as Potentate of the Zem Zem Temple he had initiated plans for a ceremonial that was scheduled to be held in Warren on September 17. Did he somehow feel that he might not live long enough to testify and he therefore made sure his testimony would be heard? Was he that certain about what was said that morning between himself and Judge Arird that he was determined to deliver his statement—even from the grave?

Miss Baldensperger was the first to take the stand. She was called as a witness for the appellants, Senauskas and Polens, by Attorney Hampson. He established for the court that she was the late MacDonald's secretary, and as such did all his typing, filing, and managed his office.

"Miss Baldensperger," Hampson began, "tell the court what happened regarding this *ex parte* affidavit."

"I typed and notarized an affidavit for Mr. MacDonald," the secretary began. "The affidavit stated that before court began on June third, 1936, Mr. MacDonald met with Judge D.U. Arird in the judge's chambers and that Judge Arird assured him that if Mr. Senauskas pleaded guilty he would not get the death penalty. I also typed and notarized an affidavit made by Mr. MacDonald to a petition by Mr. Cohen."

On cross-examination by Schofield, attorney for the Commonwealth, Miss Baldensperger admitted that she had not made a record of the affidavits, as required by law.

"It was an oversight on my part," the secretary answered in a nervous voice.

"Where are those affidavits now?" Schofield asked.

"They're in Mr. MacDonald's office."

The next witness for the appellants to take the stand was Cleveland attorney William H. Consul. Consul explained that he was attorney for Joe Senauskas' stepfather and mother, who lived in Cleveland and that he had accompanied the parents to Warren to aid in their son's defense.

"Please tell the court, Mr. Consul, what happened on the day in question," Hampson began.

"Mr. MacDonald and I went to the courthouse on the morning of June third. MacDonald went into the judge's chambers and remained there for a short time. When he came out he told me that he had assurance that if Senauskas pleaded guilty he would not be sent to the electric chair," Consul said. "After that it was decided that Senauskas would change his plea to guilty."

If anyone in the courtroom was wondering why Judge Arird had had to go all the way to Philadelphia to procure an attorney, they found out soon enough when Attorney Schofield cross-examined Consul. Schofield attacked Consul on a number of points as to what exactly had happened during the court session on June 3. On some points he was able to confuse Consul. But after a lengthy cross-examination Schofield was not able to get Consul to waver in his statement that MacDonald told him on that June morning that there was a deal in place with Judge Arird.

After Consul was excused there was a discussion as to whether other witnesses might testify as to what MacDonald had told them regarding that fateful morning in Judge Arird's chambers. But Judge Brownson would not allow such testimony, citing that it would be hearsay.

After a long morning, court recessed for lunch a little before one in the afternoon. When court resumed, Polens' attorney A.L. Cohen took the stand to substantiate his claim that the only reason Polens pleaded guilty was because he was given to understand that Judge Arird would show leniency in return for his guilty plea.

Cohen relived his version of that June day in court: "I arrived late at court, around eleven in the morning. I spoke with MacDonald then I apologized to Judge Arird for being late. I left the courtroom and went into Judge Arird's chambers, and it was in this setting that the conversation took place. I told him that I had talked to MacDonald and he told me that he was advising his client to plead guilty because of a promise of leniency.

"I then asked Judge Arird if he would give my client the same consideration and he said he would. I said I would go and talk to my client and see if he would plead guilty as well. To that, Judge Arird said 'suit yourself.'"

Attorney Schofield then began his cross-examination of Cohen.

"Mr. Cohen, did Judge Arird make any promises to you," the Philadelphia lawyer asked.

"No, he didn't," Cohen responded.

"Mr. Cohen, can you tell the court what exactly was said and by whom?"

"MacDonald told me that Judge Arird told him that he 'would show every consideration if circumstances to mitigate the crime were shown,'" Cohen said.

An open animosity was growing between Cohen and Schofield and Schofield's next venue of questioning would exacerbate the already raw feelings between the two attorneys.

"Mr. Cohen," Schofield began, "are you a member of the Allegheny County Bar Association?"

"Yes."

"Have there been any complaints filed against you with the grievance committee?"

"Yes."

"Would you tell the court how many?"

"I'm not sure," Cohen hedged. "Some have been dismissed."

"Could the number be seventeen complaints?"

"It could be. But like I said, some have been dismissed."

In point of fact, seventeen claims had been filed and eleven of them had been dismissed. The remaining six were still pending.

Continuing with his blistering cross-examination, Schofield was able to get Cohen to admit that, even before the trial began, he had considered entering a guilty plea for his client, John Polens. It was established that Cohen had spoken to Warren County District Attorney Eddy about such a plea.

The next witness called by the appellants was Joe Senauskas. Asked why he pleaded guilty he responded: "Well, Mr. MacDonald told me that if I pleaded guilty, leniency would be shown."

On cross-examination by Schofield, Senauskas admitted that even before the trial had started, he had decided to plead guilty.

"Well then, Mr. Senauskas," Schofield asked, "why did you plead not guilty when you were arraigned?"

"Mr. MacDonald told me to."

The next witness for the appellants was John Polens, and as had been happening all along in the proceedings, he more or less, repeated what Senauskas had said. He said he pleaded guilty because he was promised leniency.

Polens was the last witness for the appellants.

On the afternoon of October 27, 1936 Philadelphia Assistant District Attorney L. B. Schofield began the case for the Commonwealth. His first witness was E. H. Wicks, a Pittsburgh attorney who was chairman of the grievance committee for the Allegheny County Bar Association. Wicks confirmed earlier testimony brought up during Schofield's cross-examination of Cohen that the Bar Association had in fact received seventeen complaints regarding Cohen's conduct.

Cleveland detectives Martin P. Cooney and Mason Nichols were the last witnesses called that day. They testified that Senauskas had a bad reputation and was well known to police in Cleveland.

The hostility that had been developing between Cohen and Schofield had, by the end of the detective's testimony, escalated into a shouting match. Each attorney raised numerous objections against the other's line of questioning and when the inevitable argument ensued it was followed by sarcastic remarks shouted from one attorney to the other.

When Judge Brownson smacked his gavel down for the last time that day, he ended one of the most contentious and antagonistic days in Warren County trial history. After listening to the incessant squabbling between the two attorneys, it seemed as though the trial revolved around one attorney getting the upper hand on the other. Somehow, the fact that two men were on trial for their lives, had been relegated down the scale of importance.

The next morning, Wednesday, October 28, decorum entered the courtroom once again as eighty-five-year-old Warren County President Judge D.U. Arird took the stand for the Commonwealth. The Judge made a general denial of all the statements previously made that he had ever given any intimation that leniency would be shown Senauskas and Polens if they entered pleas of guilty to the murder of Metro Seminuk.

On direct examination by Commonwealth Attorney Schofield the Judge related his version of what had happened in his chambers on June 3, 1936 during the conversation with Attorney MacDonald: "Before Court opened MacDonald came to my chambers and asked me how to proceed with the Senauskas case. I told him that he was appointed to represent Senauskas and it was up to him to proceed the best way he saw fit.

"MacDonald then asked me if he presented a motion for withdrawal of the not guilty plea, would I accept it. I told him I would not. But, if he went into open court and the defendant asked to withdraw the plea, it would be granted."

Schofield asked, "What happened next?"

"He seemed satisfied with what I had told him and he said it would be all right," Judge Arird stated.

"Judge Arird," Schofield asked, "what if anything was said about the degree of the sentence or about the sentence itself."

"Not one word was said about it by me—or MacDonald. " Judge Arird stated. Then he added, "I never gave any intimation to anyone as to what decision would be given regarding the degree or sentence before the pleas were entered by the two men."

Next, Schofield asked Judge Arird to tell the court his version of what had happened on the morning of June 3, 1936 in his courtroom and chambers after he had spoken with Macdonald.

"We were selecting jurors when Senauskas asked to withdraw his plea of not guilty and enter a plea of guilty. The court accepted his plea and at this point we were ready to proceed with the Polens case. Cohen was not present so we had to wait. We waited all morning for Cohen to appear. When he didn't show by eleven o'clock, we decided to take a recess. Cohen arrived just before the recess was called."

"Judge Arird," Schofield asked, "I draw your attention to Attorney Cohen's testimony yesterday that shortly after he arrived in court that day you and he had a conversation about his client in your chambers. Did that alleged conversation take place?"

"No." Arird was emphatic. "There was no meeting in my chambers and no conversation."

Moving on to a new line of questioning, Attorney Schofield then asked Judge Arird if there had been another occasion when MacDonald had come to his chambers.

"Yes. After Senauskas had been sentenced he came to my chambers and asked me to a sign a petition that asked a rule to show cause that the testimony be transcribed and that MacDonald be permitted to file additional exceptions."

"And did you sign it?"

"No. I did not."

"Was there another time when MacDonald came to your chambers?"

"Yes. He asked me to sign an order for additional compensation."

"And did you sign it?"

"No. I did not."

At this point Attorney Cohen took up the cross-examination of Arird and went right to the conversation that he said took place in Arird's chambers on the morning of June 3. When asked about it, Judge Arird adamantly denied that any such conversation had taken place.

"There was no such conversation," Arird told the attorney and the courtroom. "The only thing I recall was Mr. Cohen saying on one occasion 'Polens is guilty as the devil and he has no defense.'"

Cohen then attempted to enter into evidence reports that Judge Arird was subject to lapses of memory.

"Objection!" Attorney Schofield yelled as he jumped to his feet. "Your honor there is no basis."

A shouting match between the two attorneys erupted and Judge Brownson had to intervene. After hearing both sides of the argument, Judge Brownson ruled that Cohen could not offer this evidence at this time, but upon further substantiation, he could enter the evidence at a later time.

Judge Arird had spent the morning on the witness stand and was finally excused as a witness just before the court recessed for lunch.

The first witness called by Commonwealth Attorney Schofield when the court convened at 1: 45 was Jay V. Blair, court prothonotary and clerk of the courts. Blair read the entries in the docket for June 3, showing the time that court convened on that day and also showing the actions taken by the court.

Blair corroborated Judge Arird's statement that there had never been a conversation between Arird and Cohen on the day in question. "I walked out of the courtroom directly behind Cohen." Blair stated. "I went down the stairs to the first floor, still ahead of Cohen and I turned and saw that Cohen walked directly out the front door of the courthouse."

Blair then testified that on June 27—two days after MacDonald had created his *ex parte* affidavit. "MacDonald asked me to sign the court order attached to his petition, but I refused to sign it."

"What happened next?" Schofield asked.

"MacDonald wrote an order on the petition and signed it himself."

"Objection!" Cohen jumped to his feet and another shouting match took place, and once again Judge Brownson had to intervene.

Attorney Hampson opened the cross-examination by asking Blair if he had signed an affidavit that set forth facts as given in his testimony, and if that affidavit was attached to an answer filed with the supreme court by District Attorney L.C. Eddy. Blair responded that he had signed the affidavit.

Attorney A. L. Cohen began his cross-examination of Blair. It was obvious that Cohen was trying to get Blair to change his testimony about Cohen's alleged visit with Judge Arird. Cohen asked, "Mr. Blair, can you remember events that happened on, say, June first or June tenth?"

"I don't know what you mean. I suppose I could. I'm not sure," Blair responded.

"Well then, how is it Mr. Blair that you can recall the events of June third so vividly?"

"Objection!" Hampson was on his feet. Another shouting match ensued and Judge Brownson once again disengaged the attorneys and brought order to the courtroom. It was obvious that Cohen was trying to get Blair to admit that the only reason Blair remembered the events that day as he did was because Blair was in fact trying to aid his friend, Judge Arird.

But Blair stuck with his version of events that day: that being that Cohen did not meet with Judge Arird on June 3.

The Commonwealth then called Miss Alta E. Lund, court stenographer. "MacDonald came into the Judge's chambers and they did talk, but no promises were made to MacDonald at that time. Nothing was said concerning any sentence which might have been imposed on Senauskas." Miss Lund delivered her testimony in such an emphatic way that she left little doubt that—as far as she was concerned—what she said was exactly what had happened.

Schofield then called a surprise witness, Miss Alice Mead, Judge

Arird's niece. She testified that on June 3, Judge Arird came home for lunch at 11:15 in the morning.

Schofield then called the court crier, Frank V. Conarro. "Mr. Conarro, would you tell the court what happened on the morning of June third regarding your and Judge Arird's movements?"

"I accompanied the Judge from his home to the courthouse that morning and I was with him when the noon recess was called and we went to his niece's home for lunch."

"Did you see Mr. Cohen go into the Judge's chambers that morning?"

"No."

"Can you tell the court what else happened that morning?"

"After Senauskas pleaded guilty, we tried to find Mr. Cohen."

"Were you successful?"

"No. No one knew where he was until he entered the courtroom at about 11 that morning."

"Court adjourned," Judge Brownson called out as he simultaneously brought his gavel down hard.

CHAPTER XI

Day Three of the petition hearing brought forth by confessed murderers Joe Senauskas and John Polens against Warren County President Judge D.U. Arird and the Commonwealth of Pennsylvania began on the morning of Thursday, October 29, 1936.

The first witness called was Frank V. Conarro, court crier, who was on the stand the previous afternoon when court was adjourned. Attorneys Hampson and Cohen, attorneys for the appellants, both centered their cross-examination on Conarro's credibility as a witness.

The next witness was eighty-year-old James H. Berger, the court tipstaff[2]. Berger went into great detail about efforts that were made on the morning of June 3 to find Attorney Cohen. Berger corroborated Conarro's testimony point-by-point that Cohen did not meet with Judge Arird that morning and that no conversation between Cohen and Arird had taken place.

The next witness was Corporal Joseph F. Schmidt of the Pennsylvania State Police, stationed at the Hershey barracks. Schmidt told the court that at the time of the murder he was stationed at the Kane barracks and was one of the principal investigators in the case.

Commonwealth Attorney Schofield asked Schmidt to tell the court what happened in court on the morning of June 3 and days surrounding that date.

"Senauskas was brought into court and there was a very brief conference held in the law library before the court opened. Senauskas, MacDonald, and Consul were present."

65

Schofield then asked, "Corporal Schmidt, Attorney Consul stated in previous testimony that this conference was held after the court had opened. Is that true?"

"No." Schmidt stated. "The conference was held before the court was open. I'm certain of that."

"Could you tell the court, Corporal Schmidt, what if anything happened on the afternoon of June second, 1936?"

"There was a conference held on the afternoon of June second. I was there. Police officers Sergeant E. J. Donovan and Sergeant Price and Private Mehallick of the state police were there. MacDonald and Consul were there with their client Joe Senauskas."

"And what if anything did Joe Senauskas say that day?" Schofield asked.

"Senauskas said that it was his intention to plead guilty—to throw himself on the mercy of the court," Schmidt said, ending his testimony.

State Police Sergeant E. V. Donovan of the Butler barracks was then called to the stand. Donovan corroborated Schmidt's testimony and the lunch recess was called. When court convened that afternoon, Donovan was back on the stand. Under cross-examination by Cohen he added that the only further information he could offer about the case was that Attorney Macdonald had written a letter to the Butler barracks asking that there be a conference with the state police regarding the Senauskas case.

The next witness called by the Commonwealth was Deputy Sheriff William Stuart. Stuart testified that after the June 2 meeting wherein Senauskas and MacDonald decided to plead guilty the next day in court, Attorney Cohen said to him: "That puts me on the spot."

"Is there anything else you can offer," Schofield asked.

"There were a number of times when Senauskas told me that he just wanted to get it over with."

Appellant Attorney Hampson then cross-examined Stuart. "Did Joe Senauskas ever say that he intended to plead guilty?"

"No," Stuart answered.

"Isn't it a fact that all Senauskas ever said to you was that he didn't want to stand trial and he wanted to get it over with as quickly as possible?"

"Yes." Stuart ended his testimony.

Warren County Sheriff John Berdine was called to the stand next.

"Sheriff Berdine," Schofield began, "please tell the court what happened on or about June third of this year. Did you see attorney Cohen?"

"When I escorted John Polens back to the county jail when court was over, Attorney Cohen was not with Polens."

"Sheriff, did Joe Senauskas ever tell you that he wanted to plead guilty to the murder of Metro Seminuk?"

"Yes." Sheriff Berdine said, "When Senauskas was told that MacDonald was appointed by the court as his lawyer, he stated to me that he didn't want a lawyer and that he would rather plead guilty and throw himself on the mercy of the court."

The next witness called by the Commonwealth was Warren County Jail Warden Ernest Berdine.

"Did Joe Senauskas ever tell you that he wanted to plead guilty to the murder of Metro Seminuk?" Schofield began.

"No. He never said that to me," Berdine answered. "I escorted Senauskas back to jail after court that day. MacDonald walked with us but Senauskas never said he didn't want MacDonald as his lawyer. The only thing MacDonald said was that he had a severe headache and needed to get away from the courtroom."

But on cross-examination by Hampson for the appellants another story emerged.

"Warden Berdine, did you ever tell my client Joe Senauskas that he should plead guilty to the murder of Metro Seminuk?" Hampson asked.

"Yes. I told him that it would be best for him to plead guilty and take his chances on the mercy of the court," Warden Berdine admitted.

But on redirect questioning by Schofield, Berdine said: "I made those statements in response to questions from Senauskas as to what he should do."

Schofield called his next witness, Warren County District Attorney Leroy Carroll Eddy.

"Mr. Eddy, did you have any conversations with Attorney MacDonald or Attorney Cohen regarding their defense of Joe Senauskas and John Polens?"

"Yes. Both Mr. MacDonald and Mr. Cohen, more or less intimated to me that their clients might plead guilty."

"Mr. Eddy, was there any time after that when Mr. MacDonald talked to you again about his client's plea?"

"On the afternoon of June second, Mr. MacDonald told me to take my time in picking a jury for Senauskas, as he might enter a plea of guilty."

"Mr. Eddy, were there other occasions when Mr. Cohen spoke to you about the case against his client John Polens?"

"Yes. Mr. Cohen told me on one occasion that he had investigated the case against John Polens and that he knew when he was up against a stone wall," Eddy said. "On another occasion, I believe May sixteenth, Cohen assured me that Polens would plead guilty."

When Schofield finished with Eddy, Cohen jumped to his feet and began his cross-examination of the district attorney. He would have been better off staying in his seat.

"Mr. Eddy, isn't it true that I never said that my client would plead guilty? Didn't I say that I would only advise my client to plead guilty?"

This was a bad move on Cohen's part, because when the District Attorney responded, he left little doubt as to what Cohen had said or what he thought of the questionable tactics of the lawyer who had had a number of grievances filed against him.

"No, Mr. Cohen, I'm positive beyond any doubt that you told me your client would plead guilty," Eddy replied. "In fact, Mr. Cohen, you even promised me John Polens would plead guilty."

Three of the five jurors who had been seated in the courtroom on June 3, testified as to what they saw that day. Those jurors were Mrs. Mabel Pearson of Russell, Mrs. Edna Clarke of Youngsville, and J. A. Aaron of Warren. Two reporters—Elwyn W. Hildum and W.R. Walsh—testified as to what they witnessed that day. They all agreed that during the proceedings Joe Senauskas and his attorney, Earle MacDonald, stood and informed the court that Senauskas wanted to change his plea from not guilty to guilty.

***

Private John Mehallick was called as the next witness for the respondents. And as soon as Schofield began his direct examination, it was clear what Schofield's motive was, and it also became clear why Private Mehallick had returned to Warren on October 14, thirteen days before the trial was to begin.

"Private Mehallick," Schofield said, " did you travel to Pittsburgh and conduct an investigation as to the character of Attorney Cohen? And if so, please tell the court what you learned as a result of this investigation."

"A number of people I questioned did not think very highly of Mr. Cohen."

At this, Cohen burst into a rage and the two attorneys yelled insults to each other until Judge Brownson once again established order. But strangely this blatant attempt to discredit Attorney Cohen didn't work out very well. On cross-examination Sergeant Mehallick admitted that he only questioned a few people; and it was further discovered that these people had reasons to dislike Cohen.

Cohen made a motion that Mehallick's testimony be stricken from the record and Judge Brownson agreed to take the motion under advisement.

The next witness called for the Commonwealth was Private S.C. Banks, also a state police officer. Banks, who was also present in the courthouse on June 3, corroborated the testimony of his fellow officers. But, on cross-examination, he did bring up a troubling point for the Commonwealth.

"Corporal Schmidt had gone to the county Jail with Polens after the 11 o'clock recess. I had not seen Cohen all morning."

Hampson immediately recognized the inconsistency. Previously, Corporal Schmidt testified that he spoke with Cohen when Cohen entered the courtroom at 11 o'clock. But Bank's testimony placed Schmidt out the door of the courthouse before Cohen ever came in the courthouse.

Also, Polens testified earlier that he was not in court that morning. He stated in previous testimony that Cohen did not come to his cell until between 11:30 and noon. Was Polens' version the correct account? Was it that there were so many state police in the courthouse that day that sooner or later a discrepancy in their accounts would emerge?

The last witness of the day was Sergeant E.J. Price of the Butler barracks of the state police. Price told of the meeting he saw and heard after the June 2 meeting of the late Earle MacDonald and Senauskas. He corroborated what the other Commonwealth witnesses stated—that after that first meeting between Senauskas and MacDonald, MacDonald said that his client wanted to plead guilty.

However, Schofield on redirect posed the question to Officer

Price that could it have been possible since all the officers—except Schmidt—were at the front door and that Schmidt was in the rear corridor, that Schmidt might have gone out one door while Cohen came in another. Price offered that it was possible.

But, that still doesn't clear up the discrepancy that Schmidt said he spoke to Cohen when Cohen came into the courtroom at 11 o'clock.

If Price had indeed thrown a curve to the Commonwealth, he more than made up for it when he related a conversation he'd had with Joe Senauskas. Before the now famous meeting in the law library between MacDonald and Senauskas and half-dozen police officers, when Price and Senauskas were sitting in court, Price said Senauskas leaned over to him and said that he was going to plead guilty. Price quoted Senauskas' next statement, "'They're going to burn me so why waste all this time.'"

Price said he then informed MacDonald of what Senauskas had said and a recess was called, whereupon all the players, including Cleveland Attorney William Consul and the police officers, went into the law library.

Price continued, "When I told MacDonald that Senauskas wanted to change his plea to guilty, MacDonald said 'It's his funeral, not mine."

"It was finally decided that day in the law library that they would continue to choose jurors and that they would withhold their decision until the following day, June third."

From the scope of his testimony, it appeared that Price had spent more time with Senauskas than other officers. He continued his testimony. "Senauskas told me that Consul was a "fixer" from Cleveland and that he told his father to send Consul back to Cleveland. There was nothing he could do here."

Price related yet another occasion when Senauskas admitted his guilt. "We were riding from the Butler barracks to Corry to pick up the gun he used to shoot Seminuk. He said during that trip that he intended to 'take the rap.'"

On cross-examination by Hampson, Price said that he visited Senauskas and Polens in the county jail after they were sentenced and Senauskas said to him 'They can burn me at any time.'"

"What did you reply?" Hampson asked.

"I wished him luck."

Price was still on the stand when the court was to adjourn. He had one more anecdote. "We were at the Kowalski farm at Colza near Corry, when Senauskas was saying goodbye to his girlfriend, Katherine Kowalski. Senauskas said he would see her in about two weeks. Miss Kowalski replied, 'You will like hell. You'll see me like Bruno Hauptman[3]'."

***

Day Four began on the morning of Friday, October 30. The Commonwealth called its first witness, Sergeant E. J. Price of the Butler barracks of the state police. Price was the last witness Thursday and had finished being questioned on direct examination by Schofield. This morning attorneys for the appellants would conduct more cross-examination. Hampson's questions centered on the events of June 2 and 3. After prolonged questioning regarding the meetings that took place on those days, Hampson moved on to a new line of questioning, something that had not been brought up before.

"Sergeant Price," Hampson approached the witness, "On April eighth of this year, did you take a signed confession from John Polens?"

"Yes sir."

"At the time of this confession, did you promise Polens that you would help him in his case if he signed the confession?"

"No sir, I didn't."

At this point Price stepped down and Cohen called Sergeant E.J. Donovan and asked him the same questions that Hampson had asked Price.

Donovan responded that he did not make any promises, but that he had said, "I suggested to Senauskas there was nothing for him to do but enter a plea to the charges."

If anyone observing or involved in the Senauskas/Polens plea for a new trial thought that the worst of the lawyer haggling and wrangling was behind them, they were in for a shock as Day Five began with a bang on Saturday morning, October 31.

Attorney L.C. Cohen for the appellants led off the morning by calling local attorney Richard P. Lott to the stand. It was becoming clear to everyone—Cohen included—that he had not been able to break down any of the Commonwealth's witnesses' testimony that there had been no conversation between himself and Judge Arird on the morning of June 3.

71

It was his word against Judge Arird's and a handful of court and police personnel.

But in reality, it all boiled down to Judge Arird's word against Cohen's word. Because, regardless of what testimony Commonwealth witnesses gave, there were only two people who knew beyond all doubt whether or not a conversation had actually taken place that morning: Cohen and Judge Arird. And, if there was indeed a conversation, only Arird and Cohen knew beyond all doubt what was said.

Thus did Cohen devise a plan to discredit Judge Arird's testimony.

Cohen's plan was at once bold and foolhardy. Seeing the direction the hearing was taking and sensing that, not only did the state have credible witnesses but also the appellants really had no case beyond the alleged plea bargain, he decided to attack the core of the matter. It can only be assumed that the Pittsburgh attorney's mindset at this point was, What have we got to lose?

On that October morning, on the fourth day of the trial, with time running out, Cohen made the decision to question whether Judge Arird's memory was faulty. Here, as the saying goes, the plot thickens: Where did Cohen get this idea in the first place? Who planted this seed in his head? Did someone have a resentment against Judge Arird, who was considered by some as arrogant? Did Cohen overhear a chance remark at dinner in a local restaurant? Did someone that the judge had ruled against in a previous trial slip a note under the door of Cohen's hotel room door?

How did a man who lived and practiced law in Pittsburgh become privy to such alleged knowledge? And, of course, there remained one crucial question, perhaps the most important question regarding all the legal proceedings that had taken place since Senauskas and Polens were arrested: Was Judge Arird's memory faulty? And, if it were, what local attorney would have the chutzpah to broach the subject with His Honor?

It's easy to imagine the scenario that if indeed the judge's memory were failing, the common consensus among local law enforcement and court personnel could have been: He's had a distinguished career that no one wanted to besmirch; let's just let him ride out his tenure and pray to God that nothing serious comes before him and that sooner or later, the Old Boy will retire.

But, obviously, those who may have harbored those thoughts were now witnessing their worst nightmare coming into fruition.

Cohen began his questioning of Lott by establishing that Lott was a local attorney and had occasion to have dealings with Judge Arird.

"Mr. Lott, was there ever an occasion when you had dealings with Judge Arird when you questioned his memory?"

"Objection," Schofield sprung to his feet.

For the next two hours Cohen and Schofield shouted at each other and ranted that each was correct in his thinking. Once again, Judge Brownson disentangled the two combatants and was able to move the trial forward.

Lott was asked numerous questions about his law career to establish his credibility. He was then allowed to relate the specific instances were he felt Judge Arird's memory was faulty. He ended his testimony by saying, "I would say the judge is forgetful."

Cohen's grand scheme had come in like a lion and gone out like a lamb, with a lone witness. Undeterred, Cohen switched strategies and called his next witness, local attorney R. Pierson Eaton. Cohen's first question to Eaton asked Eaton to tell the court about the reputation of the late Earle MacDonald as one who was honest.

Judge Brownson stopped Eaton's testimony and had him withdrawn as a witness. He explained, "In the absence of any attack on MacDonald's reputation, his reputation for truth and veracity would be considered good."

Cohen called his next witness, John Polens. "John, did you and I have a discussion on the morning of June third?"

"Yes, we did," Polens responded.

Cohen offered Polens' testimony in rebuttal to previous testimonies by court and sheriff's personnel that he and Polens had had no conversation that morning.

"Would you tell the court if any police officers made any promises to you?"

"They gave me assurance that they would try to get my sentence reduced to ten years and also they would not oppose a pardon."

"Tell the court where you were on the morning of June third."

"I was not in court like those witnesses said. I was still in my jail cell until you came for me maybe between 11:30 and 12:00."

Schofield then took up his cross-examination. "Mr. Polens isn't it a fact that you were planning on pleading guilty and that you would have, regardless of what the officers said?"

"At one time, yes."

"Also, Mr. Polens, you were once a justice of the peace and you're a college graduate. Surely you knew that those officers could not make any promise that leniency would be shown. You knew that, didn't you, Mr. Polens?"

"Yes."

After the noon recess, Attorney Hampson continued his effort to present witnesses to testify as to the character and credibility of the late Earle MacDonald. Judge Brownson repeated to Hampson what he had ruled on this matter the day before. "Mr. Hampson, inasmuch as the standing and reputation of Mr. MacDonald has not been attacked, it is not necessary to call witnesses."

Judge Brownson's point here is that since no one has come forward and stated anything negative regarding the integrity and veracity of the late Earle MacDonald, it wasn't necessary to provide witnesses to prove as much. In short, the court acceded that MacDonald was a truthful and honest attorney. But Hampson was not appeased.

In the end, the two jurists reached a compromise. MacDonald's character witnesses would not testify but their names would be entered in the court records: William Glassman, Ethel Baldensperger, Judge E.S. Lindsey, and Harold Hampson.

Sheriff John Berdine was recalled to the stand in an effort to answer the question as to what had happened to the $70 Senauskas had in his possession at the time of his arrest. Berdine said that he never handled the money, that it was returned to Senauskas by Deputy Sheriff Stuart after a discussion with District Attorney Eddy.

Joe Senauskas was recalled to the stand and stated that he had received the money from the deputy sheriff. When asked what he did with it, Senauskas replied, "I gave part of it to my step-dad and kept the rest for myself."

Appellant Attorney Cohen addressed the court and recalled Court Prothonotary J.V. Blair. Cohen asked that the court docket be produced and he then questioned Blair at length on a number of the entries on the docket. Cohen then asked that Blair's original notes be produced and the docket and the notes were entered as exhibits in the case. Cohen told the court he wanted the documents in evidence because he wanted to go over them and compare the notes with the entries on the docket. He added that he also wanted to study the handwriting.

Attorney Schofield then put on the stand six Warren county attorneys who testified that Judge D.U. Arird had an excellent memory: Allison D. Wade, William I. Glassman, Warren Stone, Major C.E. Bordwell, W.S. Clark, and District Attorney L. C. Eddy.

Attorney Cohen then cross-examined Wade, Stone, Bordwell, and Clark. These were the last testimonies taken in the hearing.

Judge Brownson called for a sidebar with the Commonwealth and appellant attorneys. He informed the attorneys that the hearing was ended and that he estimated that it would require a month to complete the transcript of the five days of testimony. He added that because of the approaching holiday season and other pending court matters, the next phase of the case—the arguments—would not be heard until after the first of the next year.

Thus ended what was sure to be remembered as one the most sensational and contentious hearings ever held in Warren County.

As the attorneys packed their briefcases, it's difficult to imagine what they must have felt. The case had, by no means, tilted significantly in one direction or another. The matter of the alleged June 3 meetings that Judge Arird had first with MacDonald and later with Cohen was left unsettled. Certainly both Arird and MacDonald had impeccable reputations.

Cohen, of course, was the wild card. But even if Judge Brownson threw out Cohen's statement, he was still left with the one question that went to the heart of the matter: Did MacDonald and Judge Arird make a deal or not?

Did Appellant Attorneys Hampson and Cohen prove to Judge Brownson that MacDonald had a deal in place? Was there in fact any validity to the appellants' claim that their clients' confessions were coerced by a promise of leniency, by a promise that they would not go to the electric chair? Did Senauskas and Polens receive a fair trial?

Clearly, on one point the defendants had received some incredibly bad advice. Consider this: If Senauskas intended on pleading guilty and throwing himself on the mercy of the court, why didn't he continue with the jury trial? Why did he reject a trial by jury, where there would have been twelve people, some of them mothers and even grandmothers hearing his case? Why would he let a jury of his peers walk out the door and place his fate in the hands of one man—an eighty-five—year-old judge who clearly held the defendants in disdain?

Surely any lawyer, even in 1936, would have known that a defendant's chances were always better with a jury. The odds of one or a few jurors feeling some measure of sympathy for the troubled teenager were much greater with twelve unique minds considering the case than with one octogenarian judge, who had been in the legal profession since 1892 and President Judge of Warren and Forest counties since 1921.

Surely, any reasonable person would consider that to Judge Arird these two defendants were just two more lost souls in the parade of lost souls that passed through his courtroom.

Did the appellant attorneys, one appointed by the court and one travelling all the way from Pittsburgh, feel that a bench trial before Judge Arird would go faster? How did both attorneys, who later pulled out every angle they could use, make such a stupendous blunder even before the trial began?

If the attorneys involved thought they could speed the process along by agreeing to a bench trial, they were remarkably off base. Essentially, the trial and preparations for the trial and the subsequent hearing had already lasted seven months and the end, unbeknownst to everyone involved, was nowhere in sight. There was no light at the end of the tunnel; in fact, at this point, there was not even a tunnel in sight.

Of course, Senauskas and Polens had no idea of how long they would be held in limbo. They had no idea how long they would live with a death sentence hanging over them. Like everyone else, the two confessed killers would have to learn to wait while the wheels of justice turned ever so slowly.

The only thing that Senauskas and Polens were reasonably sure of at this stage of the procedure was that nothing would be done until the early months of 1937. There was one immutable fact that the men did know: they would be eating turkey dinner at Thanksgiving and celebrating Christmas 1936—perhaps their last—as guests of Warren County.

CHAPTER XII

Sixty-one days after Judge James I. Brownson of Washington County concluded the five-day hearing of appellants Joe Senauskas and John Polens in their quest for new trials he was back in Warren County. On the morning of Tuesday, January 5, 1937, Brownson opened the arguments phase of the proceedings.

The Judge's first announcement was that A.L. Cohen, attorney for John Polens, would not be in court. Brownson informed the court that Cohen had filed a written brief of his arguments in the case and had it delivered to him.

Attorney Harold Hampson, court-appointed attorney for Joe Senauskas, began the session with his argument before the court. Perhaps, wishing to diffuse some of the acrimony and name-calling that had been rampant during the October hearing, Hampson offered yet another theory of how all the honorable and honest jurists, secretaries, court employees, and police personnel had testified, on some points, in direct opposition to each other; and that, even when witnesses did agree, there was still a number of inconsistencies in their testimonies.

"I don't believe anybody who took part in that hearing willfully fabricated his story," Hampson told the court. "What I believe happened is that memories proved unreliable."

Hampson said there were other cases in which he had been involved where seemingly honest persons told conflicting stories. He said it was not uncommon in courtroom proceedings.

Returning to the case at hand, Hampson gathered his notes and went directly to the heart of his client's defense. "My client testified in the hearing that he changed his plea from not guilty to guilty because Mr. MacDonald told him that the alleged promise was given by Judge Arird that if he did plead guilty, he would escape the electric chair."

At this point, Hampson made a brilliant tactical move. One—that it would seem—would please everyone involved. "It's possible that no promise was made that morning, or at any other time. But, as far as my client is concerned, he believed what his attorney told him: that there was a deal in place. My client changed his plea from not guilty to guilty because he believed his attorney, an attorney appointed to him by this court," Hampson stated to the court.

Hampson next spoke of testimony from the hearing where witnesses said that Senauskas told them that he intended to plead guilty even before the alleged deal was in place. The attorney read passages from some of the testimonies, and although the Commonwealth's witnesses related much the same thing, there were discrepancies regarding how the statements made by Senauskas were made. In other words, were the supposed statements part of an ongoing dialogue where Senauskas made these alleged statements as a result of law enforcement personnel asking him questions or offering him solicited or unsolicited advice?

Hampson next addressed Point Seven of the twenty-three points of Attorney MacDonald's original appeal to the State Supreme Court: "Judge Arird based his opinion on the degree of guilt for Senauskas' plea of guilty based on information received outside of the court record."

Hampson's concern regarding Point Seven asked this question: Did Judge Arird use information he received by talking to state police about Senauskas and his alleged criminal background, to weigh on his decision to affix the death penalty? Put another way: Would Judge Arird have sentenced another defendant without a criminal record or a bad reputation in the law enforcement community to death?

Regardless of the answers to those questions, the point remained that Judge Arird took information from sources outside the record. This alone would seem to be a clear violation of American jurisprudence.

Commonwealth Attorney L. B. Schofield began his argument with a novel idea. "Accusations by the defendants go further than an attack on a local jurist, they attack the entire judicial system."

Schofield's position seems to be that for a defendant's attorney to accuse a judge of not telling the truth and for the court to agree with the defendant would set a dangerous precedent in the American system of justice. His point seems to be that if this aspect of the Senauskas case went in favor of Senauskas, every defendant who was found guilty could somehow utilize this 'dishonest judge defense' to appeal his case. In its simplest terms, what Schofield is saying is that we must assume that judges are honest.

Schofield's next tactic was to produce an outline of the events of June 3, 1936. Schofield's interpretation of that infamous day was that the appellant attorneys' testimonies simply were not credible nor were they even possible. The Philadelphia attorney also found the defendants' original appeal to the Supreme Court to be fraught with inconsistencies.

Turning his attention to the positive side of the October hearing, Schofield told the court that the witnesses for Judge Arird were impressive indeed. In referring to the judges and lawyers who testified in Arird's behalf, he told the court: "Never have I seen an array of witnesses as I have seen here."

Schofield once again attacked the credibility and honesty of appellant Attorney A.L. Cohen. "I remind the court that Mr. Cohen took the stand at the hearing and stated that no promise of any kind had been made by Judge Arird regarding leniency for Polens, although Cohen claimed that he'd had a conversation with the judge which led him to believe he and his client would be given 'consideration,'" Schofield told the court.

Schofield then took a new tack and stated: "Neither defendant has ever denied that he took part in the murder of Metro Seminuk or that he is guilty of first degree murder."

Before he ended his argument, Schofield revisited his opening statement. As an assistant district attorney in Philadelphia, it must be assumed that Schofield felt that he had more experience in prosecuting felony cases than the Warren jurists or even Judge Brownson, who was from Washington County, an even less populous area than Warren County. Taken in this light, his argument carries more weight. In point of fact, his argument makes good sense.

"The whole system of jurisprudence is at stake in this case," Schofield warned the court, "for it involves not only the petitions of these men, but the safety of the courts from attacks by criminals who are not satisfied with the dispositions of their cases."

Warren County District Attorney L.C. Eddy spoke next. He outlined, point-by-point, the manner in which the trials of the defendants were handled. Then he stated: "There was exact regularity throughout."

On the matter of Judge Arird obtaining information about the defendants from sources outside the courtroom, Eddy told the court that the judge was 'within his rights' to gain information about the accused in this fashion. In closing, Eddy told the court, "The defendants were treated fairly and given every consideration, and what has been done should stand."

In rebuttal, Attorney Hampson reasserted his position on the fact that Judge Arird received information about the defendants from persons outside the courtroom.

"The court should not consult any person in rendering an opinion, but should rely entirely upon the witnesses and the testimony given in court," Hampson stated, then continued with his summation. "We are not here to decide the guilt or innocence of the defendants. We are here to decide whether these men should be able to withdraw their pleas and be granted a new trial. The lives of two men are at stake and every consideration should be given to them."

Metro and Mary Seminuk shortly after they were married. Metro's family had emigrated from Russia. Mary was of Rumanian descent. (Author's collection)

Chunks of ice were swept along in the torrents of water as the Allegheny River and Conewango Creek flooded their banks during the St. Patrick's Day Flood on 1936. (Warren County Historical Society)

Detectives trying to find out who killed the owner of the Airport Inn had to abandon their automobiles and enlist the aid of small boats and canoes to navigate the floodwaters. (Warren County Historical Society)

Charlotte Eriksen Hunt stands in front of the house on Old Pittsfield Road where she and her family lived when the murder took place. Her mother Emilie actually heard the shots. With her is current owner Steve Younger. (Author's collection)

Charlotte Eriksen Hunt was 16 at the time of the murder and a friend of Helen Seminuk, Metro and Mary's eleven-year-old daughter. Charlotte was subpoenaed to the trial and attended every day. (Author's collection)

Tom Bower was accustomed to walking the one mile from the family homestead on York Mountain to the Airport Inn. That night he walked to the Inn to get a can of kerosene. (Author's collection)

The Garland Inn was a popular spot where John Polens hung out. On the night of the murder, Senauskas and Polens met here. Polens stayed and drank while Senauskas drove the rented car to the Airport Inn. (Warren County Historical Society)

The Garland Inn was a clean, well-lighted place in the 1930's.
John Polens, who lived in Garland, was a regular. (Warren
County Historical Society)

The building on U.S. Route 6 that housed the Airport Inn is now a private residence. (Author's collection)

The Blue Eye Inn stands today on the site where the Garland Inn once stood. (Author's collection)

Metro Seminuk was buried in this Orthodox cemetery on U.S. Route 6, less than one-half mile from the Airport Inn. (Author's collection)

Metro Seminuk was instrumental in starting this Orthodox cemetery. He was one of the first persons buried there. (Author's collection)

The Warren County Courthouse circa 1936. (Warren County
Historical Society)

It was standing room only during the murder trial. Many spectators brought their lunches so they wouldn't lose their seats during
lunch break. (Warren County Historical Society)

The Honorable Delford U. Arird was 85 years old when the trial
started. Little did he know that he would also be on trial before
this case was finished. (Author's collection)

The Honorable James Brownson, president judge of the 27th Judicial District, was sent to Warren to find out what had really happened in Judge Arird's courtroom.

In 1935 Joseph Margiotti became the youngest attorney general in Pennsylvania history. He served one term from 1935 to 1938. When he got involved in the case, things changed.

Pennsylvania Governor George Howard Earle (left, with Margiotti) was a WWI war hero. He served one term, from 1935 to 1939. Like Margiotti, his tenure bracketed the infamous murder trial.

Western Pennsylvania Penitentiary on the North Side in Pittsburgh circa 1936. (Photo PA DOC)

Rockview State Prison in Centre County was built in 1912 to ease the overcrowded conditions at Western Penitentiary. Rockview houses "Death Row." Since 1915, all executions have been held at Rockview. (Photo PA DOC)

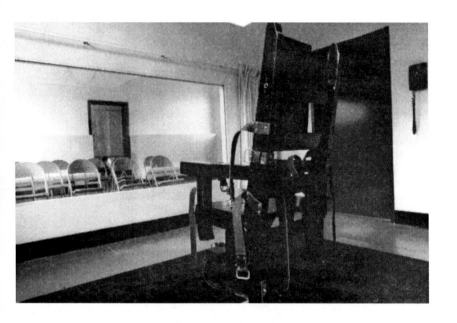

The infamous Electric Chair "Old Sparky" at Rockview. (Photo PA DOC)

Joe Senauskas was born in Hartford, Connecticut in 1916. He was 19 years old when he shot and killed Metro Seminuk.

John Polens was born in 1905 in Pittsburgh. He was a college graduate who ended up driving a cab. His doctor recommended that he move to the country to improve his well being.

CHAPTER XIII

On March 25, 1937, just one day short of the one-year anniversary of the murder of Metro Seminuk, Judge James I. Brownson returned to Warren County to deliver his decision as to whether or not Seminuk's confessed killers—Joe Senauskas and John Polens—were entitled to receive new trials. It took Judge Brownson a little over eleven weeks to evaluate the arguments of the attorneys and to review their briefs.

Although neither side knew what to expect from Judge Brownson, a letter received by Warren County District Attorney L.C. Eddy prior to the court date did state that Brownson would confine his decision to the motions of new trials. All other points brought out in the October hearing, the letter stated, would be presented directly to the Supreme Court.

If a man condemned to die in the electric chair can *in any way imaginable* be considered lucky, Senauskas and Polens had already been lucky once when their appeals to the Supreme Court in June, 1936 led to the October, 1936 and January, 1937 hearings held by Judge Brownson. They had cheated the hangman for months while they awaited Brownson's decision.

Senauskas and Polens were lucky in another respect, as well: they were going to be held in the Warren County Jail until their fates were decided. In fact, while it wouldn't be reasonable to picture Warren County deputies carrying a lighted birthday cake and singing, Joe Senauskas did celebrate his twentieth birthday in the Warren County Jail on December 21, 1936. And, as any former guest of a state prison could attest, comparing a stay in a small county jail to a maximum-security prison would be like comparing an earthworm to a rattlesnake.

About the only people who weren't lucky were the deputy sheriffs who took turns watching Senauskas and Polens—twenty-four hours a day, seven days a week for their entire stay until or if they were transferred.

The unluckiest people, however, were the taxpayers of Warren County. They had to pay for the trials, they had to pay for the Commonwealth's legal expenses, they had to pay for Senauskas' attorney Harold Hampson, and they had to pay for the overtime and extra hours deputies had to work to guard what could be called Warren County's Least Favorite Guests.

On the afternoon of March 25, 1937 Judge James I. Brownson delivered his decision on the motions of setting aside the death sentences and granting Joe Senauskas and John Polens new trials. Before a packed courtroom Judge Brownson dismissed their motions on both counts. In other words, he ruled in favor of Judge Arird and the Commonwealth.

Judge Brownson's chief reason for his decision was based on a point of law. "I have no more power than a judge regularly sitting in this court. In fact, the motions were presented too late for consideration."

The Judge's decision stunned the courtroom. And after regaining order he explained the point of law to which he was referring: "A motion for setting aside judgement and granting a new trial must be presented and acted upon during the same term of court as the sentence. The fact that no action was taken by Judge Arird to set aside the sentence or grant a new trial before the end of the June term, 1936, makes it impossible for that action to be taken now."

In handing down further opinions Brownson acknowledged that there were errors committed by Judge Arird in the two cases: "It may be here remarked that we have been impressed with the evident sincere desire and effort of the court [Judge Arird] to reach a result that would be in accordance with what is legal and just, and feel that the mention of the matters in question as having been taken into consideration has probably resulted from an unfortunate attempt to consider these cases at the same time, producing some inadvertent confusion of the evidence belonging to the respective cases."

This opinion was offered to address the appellants claims that the two cases should not have been combined and that Judge Arird accepted information from sources other than the witnesses who testified on the stand.

In connection with the charges that Judge Arird had made promises regarding the sentences, Brownson stated: "I have made my report to the Supreme Court regarding the MacDonald-Senauskas promise. Regarding the Cohen-Polens alleged promise, the weight of the evidence is against the allegation that any such promises were made by the judge."

Brownson stated that the entire matter was now in the hands of the Supreme Court and until the Supreme Court acted upon his report, no further action could be taken on either case. In what can only be called an ironic twist of fate, Brownson did admit that there were numerous reasons why he would have granted a new trial, but as he had stated in his ruling from the bench, by the time he was called in to hold the first hearing it was already too late for him to act in the matter.

In other words, Brownson is saying that after he studied the law regarding his being assigned to hold a hearing, which turned out to be held in October, 1936, he realized that in order to vacate a judgement handed down during the term that ended in June, 1936, he would have had to have ruled on that judgement before that June session was closed.

Commenting on the Senauskas case, Brownson said, "Regarding the request for arrest of judgement, this could only mean the setting aside of the sentence to the end that a new trial might be granted, such setting aside being asked for in view of the fact that sentence was pronounced before this motion was filed.

"The only matter to be passed upon in connection with the motion is the sufficiency of the reasons assigned therein, and whether they warrant and require that the sentence be vacated and a new trial granted.

"A new trial in this connection cannot mean a jury trial to determine whether the defendant is guilty or not guilty of anything, and must be treated as a retrial before the court, under the statute, for the purpose of determining whether the grade of the crime confessed by the plea of guilty was of the first or second degree, and if the former, whether the penalty should be death or imprisonment."

In his ruling on the motion that insufficient time was given between the time the crime was adjudged first degree murder and the pronouncement of the sentence, Judge Brownson stated, "In our opinion the defendant ought to have been given opportunity and time to prepare and file a motion for a new trial and reasons in support thereof.

"It is true, when defendant was asked if he had anything to say, et cetera, he or his counsel could then have asked for such time and opportunity, but if through lack of presence of mind this was not then immediately done, nevertheless we think that in a capital case the court should have withheld sentence long enough to have given the defendant and his counsel time to consider what they may wish to do in the way of moving for a new trial.

"The record shows, however, that immediately after the sentence, the defendant's counsel moved for leave to file exceptions, and this was allowed, and the present motion was filed within four days thereafter. Under these circumstances we think the motion for a new trial should have been allowed to be filed *nunc pro tunc*[4] as of a time preceding the sentence, and that sentence should have been vacated or at least suspended, to allow the motion to be considered and acted upon."

Brownson found other discrepancies. He called attention to Judge Arird's remark that *"the only kind of murder charged in the indictment was a willful, deliberate, and premeditated killing, and that the plea of guilty included an admission that the killing was of that character."*

Brownson's ruling on that statement: "The statement to this effect was unquestioningly erroneous on its face.

"It is difficult, however, to believe that the court intended to say what the words used mean on their face—that it understood the plea as having the legal effect of an admission that the killing was willful, deliberate, and premeditated, (and therefore as admitting that the offense was murder of the first degree, and thus as being in and of itself a sufficient basis to support such a finding:) for it appears that the court did, following the directions of the statute, fix a time for hearing, and did hear, testimony to show the intent with which the shooting was done, and considered, discussed and weighed the testimony; and moreover, when the statement appears in paragraph sixteen of the appendix of the opinion, it occurs in connection with consideration of a claim by defendant, made at the trial, that at the time of the shooting he was in such a condition from alcohol and narcotics, as not to be conscious of what he was doing.

"All this suggests the idea that the choice of the particular words used may have been the result of a slip of the tongue when dictating the opinion, and if so, the erroneous statement may not have worked any harm in the way of leading to a conclusion that would otherwise have been reached."

Judge Brownson listed another error made by Judge Arird. "Judge Arird's opinion shows that he took into consideration some matters not brought into the evidence presented against this defendant. It was an error to do so. A defendant in a criminal case is entitled to have all evidence that is to be considered openly produced at the trial, and to have all persons whose statements of fact are to be considered produced in such manner that he can 'meet the witness face to face' and subject their statements to the test of a cross-examination, conducted by his counsel."

Judge Brownson went over the law, which he had previously cited as the reason he could not set aside Judge Arird's sentence and grant a new trial.

"I am sitting specifically as a judge of Warren court and thus have no more power than the regular judge in that court. There is no question of the power of the court to set aside a sentence and entertain a motion for a new trial. But the power of the court to set aside, alter, or modify its final judgement, both in civil and in criminal cases, ends with the term at which the judgement was entered.

"The fact that the court chose to let the sentence stand upon the record, unchanged, and unaffected in any way by any subsequent order until after the term came to an end, appears to be, under the principal of authorities above cited, inconsistent with the existence of a power in the court, after the expiration of the term. What Judge Arird could not do after the term, I sitting in his place cannot do now."

Addressing the Polens case, Judge Brownson said that the opinion in that case followed closely that in the Senauskas case. One of the claims of the Polens motion was that the court did not consider the complete findings of Dr. Israel who acted as psychiatrist to examine Polens.

"In regard to this charge," the judge stated, "I could not find that the court failed to consider the whole of the findings."

Regarding the charge that Judge Arird allegedly expressed his opinion previous to his decision, Brownson said that this does not necessarily show error. "Judges are free to, and frequently do upon further and fuller consideration, revise and change views that they have previously expressed."

In addressing the allegation that the plea of guilty was a 'coerced' plea, Judge Brownson stated: "In our report to the Supreme Court we have found, and we now reiterate the finding here, that the weight of the evidence is against the allegation that any such promises were made by the judge, and that those allegations are negatived thereby."

Reiterating once again that he did not have the power to act on the motion, Judge Brownson stated that the errors brought up are correctable only in an appellant tribunal.

In summing up his opinion in broad strokes, Judge Brownson said: "The result of what is said above is that we find that some errors have been committed by the court, although we believe that the evidence received at the time of trial of the defendant, as a whole was sufficient to enable the court to find that the elements of murder of the first degree were established."

Immediately after the decision was read, Attorney Harold Hampson announced that the cases would be further appealed to the state Supreme Court. "In view of the errors pointed out by Judge Brownson in his opinion, there is no doubt in my mind that the Supreme Court will grant a new trial upon appeal. The only question is will it be a jury trial or a hearing before the court."

Hampson did point out that Senauskas family members were coming to Warren on Sunday and at that time he and the family would decide on a course of action.

Attorney A.L. Cohen was not present in the courtroom that day.

In response to Hampson's statement regarding the possibility of a jury trial, District Attorney L.C. Eddy said, "Without a change of plea, there could be no jury trial, but only a rehearing before a judge."

CHAPTER XIV

On April12, 1937, the Supreme Court issued its decision regarding the Brownson hearing. Chief Justice Kephart wrote: "The report of President Judge BROWNSON is most complete and covers all the matters raised by the petition, including the special assignment to pass upon the motion for a new trial as requested by the defendant. Counsel for the defendant, Earle V. MacDonald, having died, Harold S. Hampson, a member of the Warren County Bar was appointed to represent the defendant. Extensive hearings were had and 831 pages of testimony were taken. Based on this testimony the report of President Judge BROWNSON is approved."

In plain English, Joe Senauskas' and John Polens' plea for a new trial was denied and their death sentences were upheld.

In finding that there was no evidence to support the defense's assertion that a 'bargain' was entered into with Judge Arird, Kephart made public information that underscored the Commonwealth's contention that on the day in question —June 3, 1936—Attorney MacDonald's behavior was affected by his declining health.

"Counsel who then represented the defendant was in a state bordering on nervous collapse and was on that morning complaining greatly of suffering in his head, and no doubt, was then affected by the disease which later caused his death," Kephart wrote.

Kephart cited a number of other cases where it was alleged that the judge had entered into an agreement with the defense. He stated that this type of behavior would be 'judicial misconduct' and would have no binding effect, under the theory that the plea was induced by fear, promises, persuasion, or ignorance. In these cases the defendant would have the right to withdraw his plea. But, in agreeing with Judge Brownson, he found no evidence to support that Judge Arird had made any bargain.

Kephart did insert a paragraph in his findings that would serve as a way of avoiding these alleged plea-agreement fiascoes and their aftermath in the future. "Judges should not have conversations with counsel on one side relating to the disposition of a case without the presence of opposing counsel. At least, attorney for both sides should be given an opportunity to be present. This is particularly true in cases of homicide and other grave felonies, where the district attorney should always be present."

Kephart then went on to say that before petitions such as these are brought before the Supreme Court: "Allegations of judicial misconduct should be clearly proved to warrant the fastening of discredit upon any judicial officer. In the instant case, as President Judge BROWNSON found, the evidence negatives the existence of any improper conduct on the part of the presiding judge."

Kephart pointed out that there was a host of credible witnesses, such as court personnel, that supported Judge Arird's assertion that no promise had been made. He went even further and suggested that cases of this character—those with essentially no proof, should not be brought to the Supreme Court. He stated, in fact, that he thought that this case was made merely "to avoid for a time the execution of the penalty."

The judge conceded, however, that after the death sentence was imposed, no opportunity was given the defendant to file a motion for a new trial.

"A reasonable time could have been afforded defendant for this purpose. Four days later a motion for a new trial was filed which Judge Arird refused to entertain. When this matter came before Judge BROWNSON the term at which the sentence was imposed had expired. In dismissing the motion, he stated that he had no power after the expiration of the term to set aside the sentence as it was a final judgement, and as a motion for a new trial was filed after this definitive judgement, it had no effect thereon and was an unauthorized writing on the record.

"Judge BROWNSON is correct in his legal conclusion and, as he suggests, leave should have been given to file this motion *nunc pro tunc* prior to the imposition of sentence."

Essentially, what Kephart is saying is that even if defendant filed the motion for a new trial *nunc pro tunc*—now for then: filing it now as it should have been filed between the time Judge Arird found the defendants guilty and the time he affixed the death sentence, it wouldn't have changed the outcome of the Brownson hearing nor the Supreme Court's decision regarding the Brownson hearing.

"If the defendant is aggrieved by the action of the Court of Oyer and Terminer of Warren County in the finding of first degree, the imposition of the death penalty, the overruling of the motion for a new trial or any other matter, order, decree of judgement, he may take an appeal to this court, the only procedure by which this entire record may be removed here and reconsidered. We will consider at that time all matters connected therewith. The testimony which was heard by Judge BROWNSON upon the present motion will be considered as part of the record to be reviewed by us. Defendant has full opportunity to present his case to this court upon appeal, in the regular method for removal of the record by certiorari[5] to this court."

CHAPTER XV

By this time in the proceeding of the trials and appeals of Joe Senauskas and John Polens, the entire matter was beginning to take on an almost surreal aspect. John Polens' attorney A.L. Cohen hadn't been heard from in Warren for over three months, and in fact, sources close to Polens stated that he had given up on Cohen and that one of Polens' sisters had been dispatched to Pittsburgh to hire a new attorney for her brother. Polens had two sisters: Helen and Margaret.

But on May 6, 1937 Associated Press dispatches from Philadelphia reported that both Polens and Senauskas had appealed for new trials. According to the reports, Polens' appeal was filed on April 12, 1937—the same day that the Supreme Court published its decision upholding the findings of Judge James Brownson. Apparently, Polens' attorney, the errant A.L. Cohen, filed an appeal without informing his client or Senauskas' attorney Harold Hampson. The date for the Polens argument was set for May 17.

When Attorney Hampson first heard of the appeal on the morning of May 5, he quickly had Senauskas sign the necessary papers for his appeal and had them delivered to the Supreme Court in Philadelphia on the night train. The appeal reached the Supreme Court on the morning of May 6. Two days later on May 8, the Supreme Court changed the date of the hearing to Monday, September 27, 1937.

When Hampson heard of the change, he explained that ordinarily the high court sets the sixth Monday after the appeal for the hearing, but because the court would not be in session at that time, the September date had been set before the Supreme Court in Pittsburgh because the two cases were so interwoven, the court had decided to reschedule the Polens hearing to give time for him to prepare his case for Senauskas.

At this point in the ongoing drama, another new player was added: Attorney Samuel J. Goldstein, an associate of A.L. Cohen, stepped in to help with the Polens case. Goldstein, unlike his associate Cohen, did communicate with Hampson by telephone and assured the local lawyer that he believed the two attorneys should cooperate.

The only problem now was that neither attorney had the court records. Warren prothonotary J.V. Blair stated that the files were either with Judge Brownson in Washington or with the Supreme Court in Philadelphia. Blair sent a letter to locate the files and have them delivered to his office.

Five days later, on Tuesday, May 11, Prothonotary Blair received a response to his letter.

The hearings of Senauskas and Polens would be moved forward to Monday, May 24 and they would be held in Harrisburg. This news put both the men's attorneys at a distinct disadvantage. For Hampson, he had only thirteen days to prepare for the hearing and he still hadn't received the records back from the Supreme Court. Attorney Goldstein, who was new to the case, had the same predicament, plus he had very little working knowledge of the Polens case.

On Monday, May 24 prothonotary Blair announced that the Senauskas and Polens hearings had been rescheduled to be heard the week of June 7 in Philadelphia. Blair also announced that just two days earlier, on Saturday, May 22, his office received notification that Judge Arird had appointed L.B. Schofield as an assistant district attorney to assist Warren District Attorney L.C. Eddy when the Senauskas and Polens appeals went before the Supreme Court. Blair noted the order from Judge Arird had been signed on May 10.

Upon hearing that his arch-rival would once again be involved in the cases, Attorney Hampson immediately presented a petition to Judge Arird asking that the appointment of Schofield be revoked on the grounds that the Philadelphia attorney was already counsel of record for the judge and was therefore disqualified from representing the interests of the Commonwealth. Judge Arird refused to accept the petition. Hampson then filed the paper with the prothonotary's office with a notation of Judge Arird's refusal to accept it.

Once again things were heating up in the case. During the week of May 17, District Attorney Eddy went to Philadelphia to discuss matters about the case. He returned to Warren on the morning of Saturday, May 22 and met with Attorney Samuel J. Goldstein and Attorney Hampson that same afternoon.

The cases went before the Supreme Court on Wednesday, June 9 in Philadelphia. Both Hampson and Goldstein again brought up the alleged plea-agreement defense. They argued that their clients had been promised by their attorneys at the time that if they pleaded guilty to the murder charge they would not receive the death sentence.

Justice Kephart must have expected the attorneys to come up with new matter in regard to the appeal. He said that the alleged plea-agreement defense had been ruled upon during the first trial and the hearing set before Judge Brownson. In effect, he stated that the matter was settled and if either of the attorneys had anything new to bring to the table, he would listen.

To this, Attorney Goldstein replied, "I assumed that the court would hear a complete review of the entire case."

"We already know the main facts," Kephart told the attorney. "Further, the tribunal has approved the report and judgement of Judge Brownson in finding that Judge Arird had made no promises to the defendants."

However, after admonishing Goldstein for not having listed the precise questions involved in his brief, as required by the rules of the court, Kephart did allow the attorney to state his review of the case.

Then it was over. After weeks of anticipation, shattered nerves, and last-minute preparations by the defense attorneys, the hearing lasted two days. All the telegrams and telephone calls and train trips back and forth had led to this climactic—or should it be anticlimactic? —moment when Judge Kephart smacked his gavel and closed the hearing.

Joe Senauskas and John Polens had cheated the hangman for over a year now. And as far as the courts of Pennsylvania were concerned the fate that awaited them would either be new trials or a trip to Rockview Prison to keep their dates with the electric chair. The two defendants, just like everyone else in the case, would just have to wait for the decision.

***

Eighteen weeks later on October 8, 1937, the Supreme Court published its decision: the request for new trials was denied. The death sentences would be carried out. (The decision is printed in its entirety in Appendix A.)

CHAPTER XVI

It was now official: Joe Senauskas and John Polens were going to die in the electric chair in Rockview State Prison in Bellefonte in Centre County. The Supreme Court had upheld the death sentences of the two men and refused to grant new trials. All that was left to do now was the paperwork. As soon as the papers were received in Warren, from the State Supreme Court in Philadelphia, Warren County Prothonotary J.V. Blair had twenty days in which to certify the papers and deliver them to Governor George H. Earle, who would fix the date for the executions.

But on Saturday, October 16, 1937, just eight days after the Supreme Court handed down its opinion denying any further consideration to the cases, Senauskas attorney, Harold Hampson, filed a petition with that court to reopen the case and to have oral argument on the appeal heard.

In Hampson's appeal he stated that the oral argument would "give him a better chance to present the case than through the voluminous record which was used by the appellate court in reaching its decision." Within days, Polens' attorneys S.J. Goldstein and A.L. Cohen filed similar petitions.

On Saturday, November 13, 1937, the Supreme Court denied the applications.

In cases such as these, where it appears that all the defendants' avenues of escaping the electric chair have been sealed off, there is one last agency that can hear the case—the Pennsylvania Board of Pardons. The Board has the authority to commute death sentences to life in prison.

But appeals to the Board cannot be heard until the date of the execution is set by the governor. In other words, the Board cannot act on an appeal until the date of the execution is set.

By this time—over nineteen months since the murder of Metro Seminuk—the case was taking on boondoggle proportions. To members of the Warren legal community, as well as law enforcement personnel and citizenry who were following the case, the trials and the appeals seemed endless. One headline followed another and another and still another in local newspapers, as the case became the most discussed and argued case in the history of Warren County. It seemed everyone in Warren County had a different take on the case and coffee shops and kitchen klatches were the scenes of endless arguments and speculation.

But all the conversations came to an end on Wednesday, November 17, 1937 with a collective gasp as the reality and finality of the situation set in. On that day, Warren County District Attorney L. C. Eddy drove the two-hundred-and-eighteen miles from Warren to Harrisburg and personally delivered the necessary papers for execution to Pennsylvania Governor George Howard Earle.

In modern parlance, Governor George Howard Earle "caught the cases" of Senauskas and Polens. Earle's term in the Governor's Mansion neatly bracketed the infamous case, like a pair of parentheses. The Democrat began his one term in January, 1935 and it ended in January, 1939.

Earle was born December 5, 1890 in Devon in Chester County. He graduated from Harvard University and in 1916 enlisted as a private in the Second Pennsylvania Infantry, and served under General John J. Pershing in the Mexican War. He returned with a Second Lieutenant's commission. When the United States entered World War I, he enlisted and within months was promoted to command of the *U.S.S. Victor*, a submarine chaser.

On February 18, 1918, while the *Victor* was cruising the Atlantic coast with a cargo of depth bombs and a reserve supply of fuel onboard, there was an explosion in the engine room and a fire quickly spread throughout the vessel. Earle worked side by side with his men and they were able to save the ship without loss of life. For his leadership, President Wilson awarded Earle the Navy Cross.

After the war, President Franklin D. Roosevelt appointed Earle Minister Plenipotentiary of Austria. He served in Austria during one of that country's most turbulent times. He returned to America in 1934 and was elected governor of Pennsylvania the next year.

Earle was an excellent and well-known polo payer, a dog fancier and breeder, as well as an all-round sportsman. His paternal lineage could be traced all the way back to Devon, England. In this country, the Earles, who were Quakers, were leaders in politics and the banking industry. In short, the differences between the lives of the defendants and the man who held their fate in his hands couldn't have been greater. Earle was an aristocrat-sportsman-war hero, a descendant of the upright Quaker families who settled in Philadelphia and were instrumental in forming, not only the government of Pennsylvania, but of the United States as well.

The defendants were second-generation immigrants. Polens' father was born in Poland and settled his family in the rough-and-tumble "Strip District" of Pittsburgh. Polens Senior was a laborer and barely literate. Senauskas' parents came to America from Lithuania and eventually settled in what Senauskas described as the Cleveland Underworld of gangsters, bootleggers, and killers.

Governor Earle received the papers for the execution on November 17, 1937. Before the day was over, he set the week of January 10, 1938 for the executions.

***

In an interview with reporters, Senauskas attorney, Harold Hampson, stated he was pleased that the governor had set the date of the execution on the January date. This, he said, would give him sufficient time to appeal before the Board of Pardons.

On Thursday, December 2, 1937, the Board of Pardons announced that both Senauskas and Polens were issued respites from their executions until the Board had an opportunity to review the applications for commutation at the Board's January 19, 1938 meeting.

But by December 9, 1937, Frank Hean, secretary of the Board of Pardons, reported in an Associated Press story out of Harrisburg, that he had not yet received the applications of clemency for Senauskas and Polens.

"It is my understanding they will apply for commutation in January," Hean said. "The Board meets on January nineteenth and it would be necessary to obtain a respite for the pair if the plea is to be heard.

"Also, the Board has a ruling that proof of service must be signed by the trial judge and district attorney and notice of the hearing must be advertised in local newspapers for two weeks before the argument. None of this information has been forwarded to the Board, and no application has been made for the December meeting next Wednesday."

On Wednesday, December 22, 1937, Board of Pardons secretary Frank Hean announced that members of the Board were becoming concerned over the delay in the filing of the Polens and Senauskas petitions.

"Immediate action needs to be taken in order that the applications may be heard on January nineteenth, " Hean said. "The closing date to receive applications will be December twenty-eighth."

District Attorney L.C. Eddy stated that in letters dated November 21, 1937, he had advised Hampson and Cohen and Goldstein that they should prepare their appeals to the Board. He advised the attorneys that the execution date had already been moved from January 10 to January 31 in order to give the Board time to hear their appeals.

In response Attorney Hampson said he would be handling the filing of the appeals of both prisoners and that he had left the necessary papers with them to be signed. He added he was confident that he would have the appeals ready for the January 19, 1938 meeting of the Board.

On January 3, 1938 Hampson announced that he had that day filed the petitions for Senauskas and Polens. "I will appear before the Board at its January nineteenth meeting to give oral argument," Hamspon stated. If he failed in his presentation the men would be executed twelve days later on Monday, January 31, 1938.

If it's at all possible to add insult to injury in this case, the insult occurred the very next day when Mary Seminuk was seen walking and shopping in downtown Warren. Mary had served the minimum length of her sentence, eighteen months, at the Muncy Home for Women and was now a free woman. Mary, who was described as an ideal prisoner by Muncy Supervisor Florence Wilson, had been released on December 23, 1937 and had been paroled in care of her brother Mike Zurkan, who lived in Sugar Grove.

There is no record that Mary visited her former "boyfriend" John Polens in the Warren County Jail. Mary was born in 1908 and would turn thirty that first year of her freedom; her daughter Helen was born in 1925 and would be thirteen that year.

CHAPTER XVII

With the beginning of the new year of 1938 the action in Senauskas-Polens case shifted from Warren to Harrisburg, home of the Pennsylvania Board of Pardons. And although the defendants remained in the Warren County Jail, and one of their three attorneys, Harold Hamspon, lived and practiced law in Warren, what happened next would be decided over two-hundred miles away by a whole new cast of characters. Senauskas and Polens had never met the members of the Board of Pardons, and they never would.

Two days before the January 19 meeting of the Board of Pardons, Attorney Hampson took the night train to Harrisburg. This would give him the day of January 18 to fine-tune his argument. Warren County District Attorney L.C. Eddy left on the morning of January 18. Eddy told reporters that he would meet up with Philadelphia District Attorney L.B. Schofield and together they would go over the cases. Eddy stated that he would most likely argue one case and Schofield would argue the other. Defendant John Polens would be represented by yet another Pittsburgh attorney, Samuel A. Weiss, a former classmate of his at Duquesne University and a member of the Pennsylvania House of Representatives.

There were fifty-nine cases listed on the docket of the Board to be heard on January 19. The Polens-Senauskas cases were numbers six and seven and would probably be heard a little before or directly after the noon recess, if all went as planned.

But this session of the Board was not going to be—if there were such a thing at pardon hearings—just another day at the office. There were four convicted murderers who were scheduled to die, one by one, in a quadruple execution in just five days, on Monday, January 24. Their cases were to be heard during this session.

The first of these to be considered was John Oreszak. Oreszak was the youngest of three youths implicated in the murder of Floyd Tranom, an African-American motorist who was killed as he and a female companion sat parked on a lonely road in Delaware County near Chester.

Oreszak's two accomplices, Edward Rose and Theodore Duminiak, were denied appeals to the Board; their only chance of reprieve would have to be from Governor Earle.

The fourth defendant scheduled to die on the Monday morning quadruple executions was Roy Lockard of Altoona. Lockard and Margaret Karmendi were both sentenced to death after they were found guilty of killing Mrs. Karmendi's three-year-old son Matthew, Jr. with a spike. Mrs. Karmendi had received a death sentence and was twice on her way to the electric chair when she was awarded two new trials. On her third trial her sentence was changed to life in prison.

Still another death-sentence appeal was argued for Frank Stelma of Mt. Caramel, who had been convicted of killing his drinking companion, Joseph Doyle, during an argument as to where the pair was going to drink. Stelma had already won a few respites. His attorneys had argued that he was drunk when he picked up a rock and killed Doyle. His date of execution was set for Monday, February 21.

When it was his turn, Attorney Samuel G. Weiss, speaking for Polens and Senauskas, told the Board that it was unjust that a third accomplice to the murder, Mary Seminuk, was sentenced to only one-and-a-half to five years and his clients received the death penalty.

Weiss stated: "There was an understanding reached with trial Judge D. U. Arird, of Warren County, whereby the defendants would plead guilty in return for immunity from the electric chair. With this in mind, both men waived a trial by jury. But after a brief hearing on the degree of guilt, they received the death sentence."

In his clemency plea, Weiss had said nothing new, nothing that Hampson and the other attorneys had not been saying since day one. Yet something entirely different happened that day: someone in authority believed that something irregular *had happened* between the late Earle V. MacDonald and Warren County President Judge D.U. Arird in the judge's chambers on June 3, 1936.

CHAPTER XVIII

If there was one thing the Senauskas-Polens debacle didn't need it was one more captious attorney. But that's exactly what happened when Pennsylvania State Attorney General Charles Joseph Margiotti stepped into the case. Margiotti had a national reputation in criminal law and was considered one of the great trial lawyers of his day; he also was considered an expert in civil cases and in the field of appellate courts.

In his thirty-nine years as an attorney he'd handled more than one-hundred-and-fifty homicide cases, both as a defense attorney and as a special assistant to the prosecuting attorney. As a defense attorney, he lost no client to the electric chair and only two of his clients received life sentences. As a special assistant to a number of district attorneys, he won nearly all his cases and a number of those defendants were sent to the electric chair.

In the courtroom, Margiotti was like a masterful prizefighter KO-ing his opponents with one-two combinations of legal maneuvering, vicious cross-examinations, eloquent oratory, and a flamboyant showmanship. He was so successful that when other attorneys or judges or police officers got into trouble, they hired Margiotti to defend them. It didn't matter that they had been bitter opponents or from differing political parties, when their necks were on the line, they wanted Margiotti to come to their rescue.

Margiotti was born April 4,1891 in Punxsutawney to Italian immigrant parents. His father was drawn to western Pennsylvania by the lure of high-paying jobs on the railroad and in the lumber mills. In

Punxsutawney, as in most of the forested areas in the region, there were vast stands of white pine and hemlock. In "Punxsy" white pine and hemlock logs were floated down the Mahoning Creek to the Allegheny River where they were lashed together and floated downstream to Pittsburgh.

When the timber gave out, coal was discovered—or rediscovered—in the area. Coal had been discovered in the area around 1800, but its value as a commodity was nonexistent at the time because there was no way to ship it to markets outside the area. All that changed in the 1880s when a group of entrepreneurs started the Rochester & Pittsburgh Coal & Iron Company and extended the old Rochester & State Line Railroad to Punxsutawney and in a heartbeat, the Great Punxsutawney Coal Rush was on. Historians wrote that this rush for coal was on a par with the California Gold Rush of 1848.

In Punxsutawney fortunes were made and lives were changed overnight. With the influx of fortune seekers, the quiet town was changed into a bustling commercial center, with its share of greed and violence—which many times ended up in the local courtroom.

Margiotti had dropped out of school at age seventeen and was working at Weber's Clothing Store when he was called to the courthouse and asked to serve as an interpreter for two prominent attorneys who each represented an Italian-American businessman. It was thus that Margiotti got his first taste of courtroom drama. And although his family was poor, he made up his mind to go to law school and become an attorney. Prominent local business and political leaders, who saw Margiotti's potential, provided financial support.

Margiotti graduated from Indiana College of Pennsylvania in 1912. He attended the University of Pennsylvania Law School in Philadelphia, where he scored the highest marks in the University's history in Civil Procedure. In fact, his digest was so successful that another student bought the paperwork for $150 and sold it to freshmen to help them in their studies. Margiotti passed the Bar in December, 1914 and had his first murder trial in September, 1916.

In 1935 at age forty-three, Margiotti became the youngest Pennsylvania State Attorney General. He served one term until 1938 and like Governor Earle, Margiotti caught the Senauskas-Polens case.

As Margiotti stepped into the case, Warren County District Attorney L.C. Eddy stepped down as district attorney in January 1938. Eddy, would however, by special appointment, continue to prosecute the

Polens-Senauskas case for the commonwealth.

As soon as the Senauskas-Polens appeal hit the Board of Pardons at their January 19, 1938 meeting it became clear that, as the state's number one attorney, Margiotti didn't like what had transpired in this most troubling case.

His first statement to the press encapsulated his mixed feelings: "There is no question that under the facts Polens and Senauskas deserve the electric chair. But the question before us is whether they have had their constitutional rights."

Margiotti's next statement was the first time anyone in authority pressed down on the scale on the side of Senauskas' original attorney, the late Earle V. MacDonald, regarding the alleged plea agreement the attorney claimed to have made with Judge Arird.

"If Earle MacDonald swore to an affidavit you can take my word that it's correct," Margiotti told reporters.

It should also be noted at this time that it's obvious from Margiotti's remarks that he knew MacDonald. It's not clear how well he knew him but it's easy to see that he held the late attorney in very high regard. To make such a strong statement—which was in direct opposition to the Supreme Court's ruling—certainly put a whole new spin on the case. Put in simple layman's terms, we now have the State Attorney General saying there was a deal and the state Supreme Court stating unequivocally that there was no deal.

One other factor should also be mentioned at this time. Both MacDonald and Margiotti were members of fraternal organizations. In fact, they were not only members, they were leaders of these organizations, in particular the Elks.

What should have been a routine, open-and-shut case, *complete with confessions*, was now, almost two years later, one of the most troubling cases to make it to the state's top echelon of jurisprudence. No one disputed that Polens and Senauskas were guilty, but what bothered the legal community—and the Board of Pardons—was, Did the two men in fact get fair trials? Margiotti said no. State Supreme Court Justice Maxey ruled that, yes, there were irregularities in the case, but these irregularities did not affect the outcome of proceedings.

By the next day, January 21, it was clear that the Board was not going to be able to decide on the Polens-Senauskas appeal. The Board made its appeal to Governor Earle that he grant a respite on their death sentences until February 14, so that the Board could hear further evidence from attorneys on February 8. The alleged plea-agreement deal between Judge Arird and Attorney MacDonald was at the core of their deliberations.

During a press conference, Attorney General Margiotti gave voice to the heart of the dilemma. Being the state's top law enforcement official afforded Margiotti license to say what perhaps many involved in the trial wanted to say but didn't for fear of retribution. For the first time, he spoke not of the legal ramifications of the case, but the human aspect.

"There might have been an entirely human misunderstanding," Margiotti told reporters. "After all, the principals were an old man and a younger man suffering from a tumor on the brain which killed him several months later."

There was something else bothering Margiotti. He had learned that before the Judge James I. Brownson hearing an attempt was made to show the court that Attorney Harold Hampson had been told by MacDonald on the day of the sentencing that Judge Arird told him the men would not go to the electric chair.

"Judge Brownson excluded this information from the record. He shouldn't have excluded it," Margiotti stated. "The remarks MacDonald made publicly at the time would lend some weight to the case."

Margiotti added that he had notified all the attorneys involved, including Commonwealth attorney L.C. Eddy and special prosecutor L.B. Schofield, that they were to bring in affidavits from any person in Warren who was told by MacDonald that he had made a deal with Judge Arird.

When Governor Earle granted a reprieve to Senauskas and Polens he added an extra week, extending their lives until February 21. This was the governor's second reprieve and it can only be assumed that he added the additional time so that once and for all the attorneys and the Board of Pardons could settle the matter.

Polens and Senauskas were not the only convicted murderers who were granted respites after the January 19 meeting. Four other men, who were scheduled to die one-by-one in a quadruple execution at 12:30 a.m. Monday, January 31, were also spared—at least for a time—their walk down the Last Mile at Rockview. Convicted murderers John Oreszak, Edward Rose, Theodore Duminiak, and Roy Lockard would live at least another two weeks until their scheduled executions on Monday, February 14.

The special meeting of the Board of Pardons that was originally scheduled for Tuesday, February 8 was held in closed session: no attorneys were present. Apparently, Attorney General Margiotti was quick to learn that little could be gained by having the same cast of characters cover the same territory over and over again. He had a better idea.

Margiotti sent a directive to the Warren attorneys involved in the Polens-Senauskas appeal informing them that they were not to come to the Harrisburg meeting to make their arguments. They were, instead, directed to go to the Warren County Courthouse at 2 p.m. on Tuesday, February 8. On that afternoon depositions would be taken from them and any and all individuals who had any knowledge of the statements made by the late Earle MacDonald regarding the alleged, plea-agreement deal he had made with Judge Arird.

In that same directive Margiotti told the attorneys involved that the Board would not hear the case again. Any evidence the attorneys wished to have heard should be put into their depositions.

When the top lawyer of the land speaks, attorneys—even district attorneys and judges—listen. No defense or prosecution lawyers showed up at the State Board of Pardons special meeting held on Tuesday, February 8. But, apparently there was one higher authority over which Attorney General Margiotti had no control. The newest player in the Senauskas-Polens melodrama showed up at the Board's next meeting.

The Reverend Joseph H. Diamond, a Catholic priest from St. Joseph's Church in Warren, attended the February 17 meeting. Diamond had a message for the Board: "The pulse of the residents of the city of Warren are for commutation of the death sentences to life imprisonment for John Polens and Joe Senauskas. The citizens object to the death penalty because Mary Seminuk received only a short sentence and is now free."

It will never be known whether Diamond's plea did any good. But as a result of the Board's meeting that day, preparations, which were under way on Friday, February 18, to transport Polens and Senauskas to Rockview for their 12:30 a.m. Monday morning date with the electric chair were put on hold. The warden of Rockview called Warren County Sheriff J.P. Berdine with the news that Governor Earle had called and informed him that he had given the pair another month to live and that they were to remain in the Warren County Jail.

This respite, the fourth for the defendants, set their date of execution to March 21. The delay would give the Board of Pardons a month to review the depositions it received before making its decision.

But by Thursday, March 3, the Board announced that it would not be able to complete its review of the material in time and the date of the execution was changed again to Monday, April 4. This marked the fifth time the execution had been rescheduled. The Board held its regularly scheduled meeting on Wednesday, March 16, but there was no decision made regarding the case.

March 26, 1938 marked the two-year anniversary of the murder of Metro Seminuk.

On Monday, March 28, with only six days left until the scheduled executions of Polens and Senauskas, Attorney Hampson filed yet another appeal with the state Supreme Court, this time in Pittsburgh. His appeal brought nothing new to the table. He reiterated it was wrong that Judge Arird spoke privately with witnesses outside the courtroom and he again alleged that Arird had made a plea agreement with Attorney MacDonald.

However, in a press conference, Hampson did bring a new development to light: "Additional testimony in the form of depositions taken at the instance of the Board of Pardons lends credence to this fact in that a former judge of Warren County courts testified that the late Attorney Earle MacDonald, counsel for Senauskas, had told him that Judge Arird had said to him—MacDonald—that he would not sentence Senauskas to the death penalty.

"Under such facts that are becoming more clearly established, the defense should have been permitted to withdraw a plea of guilty and to proceed to a jury trial," Hampson stated.

Then the Warren attorney added an entirely new—and very significant—piece of information. "Each time I have appeared before the Pardon Board, Attorney General Margiotti has told me 'The Supreme Court should have granted you a new trial.'"

Yet on the next day after his appeal was filed, the Supreme Court ruled for the third—and final time—that it would not grant Senauskas and Polens new trials. We, of course, will never know what was in Hampson's mind on March 29, the day his third appeal was denied. But it would be a fair guess that he may have been thinking, How is it possible that the top legal minds in the state can adjudge the same case and come up with two diametrically opposed opinions?

Nevertheless, as of March 29, 1938, the Supreme Court was finished with Joseph Senauskas and John Polens.

On March 29 Hampson received a letter from the secretary of the Board of Pardons informing him that the Board had planned to meet on April 1 to decide the fate of his clients. But the meeting had been cancelled and rescheduled for April 20. Governor Earle approved the Board's change and gave the prisoners their sixth respite, fixing their new date of execution for 12:30 a.m., Monday, May 2.

With a renewed confidence Attorney Hamspon once again made the trip to Harrisburg to argue his case of commutation for Senauskas and Polens before the Board of Pardons. Warren clergyman the Reverend Father Joseph Diamond and Former Warren County District Attorney L.C. Eddy also went to the meeting. While it may have appeared on the surface that this was just one more futile mission, there was, for the first time, a distinct sense between Hampson and Eddy and Diamond that a change was in the air. Unlike the previous hearings, this hearing was the first one in which the attorneys for both sides were invited to attend by the board.

The arguments for both sides lasted an hour and a half. According to an Associated Press news release, those who attended felt that the case could go either way. One anonymous attendee stated that the prisoners had a "fifty-fifty chance."

Father Diamond stated: "All members of the Pardon Board are giving conscientious consideration to the case of the two men. They are being very scrupulous in their efforts to reach a just decision."

Attorney General Margiotti pointed out that although Father Diamond made a good point: that residents of Warren felt that the sentencing of the three defendants—with Mary Seminuk serving only eighteen months—was unjust, he stated it was not the fault of the courts.

"The fact that Polens testified at the woman's trial that she had no part in the crime, and had paid no money to have her husband killed, makes him responsible for the inequality of justice."

Secretary of the Commonwealth and Parole Board member David L. Lawrence said: "The men never had their day in court. They pleaded guilty to the murder charges on the advice of attorneys who said they would get life imprisonment."

No decision was made that day. The Board pronounced after the hearing that it would make its final decision known at its next meeting,

April 27.

Meanwhile, the Board did rule on the fate of the five other condemned murderers, whose cases had been riding the same roller-coaster ride as Senauskas and Polens over the last few months. The others were not so lucky.

Twenty-four-year-old Roy Lockard of Altoona was denied clemency. Lockard, who was found guilty of murdering 3-year-old Matthew Karmendi, Jr. with a spike, had his appeal denied. His date of execution was set for 12:30 a.m. Monday, May 2.

Twenty-year-old Wendell Forrest Bowers was also denied clemency and was scheduled to walk his Last Mile a week later on May 9. Three other youths, Edward Rose, Theodore Duminiak, and John Oreszak were found guilty of murdering an African-American motorist as he sat parked with a female companion. The youths and Lockard were scheduled to die in a quadruple execution, one after the other.

CHAPTER XIX

At its last regularly scheduled hearing on April 20, the Pennsylvania Board of Pardons made a number of decisions—in the case of four convicted murderers, final decisions. The fate of John Polens and Joe Senauskas was postponed for a week, one more time, to Wednesday, April 27. The Board at its last meeting told everyone involved that on April 27, it would—*once and for all*—-announce its final decision on the pair.

Meanwhile, two-hundred-and-eighteen miles northwest of Harrisburg, John Polens and Joseph Senauskas were doing what men with less than four days to live might be expected to be doing. And the people of the city of Warren were doing the same thing: waiting.

Visitors to the pair noted that Polens, who had been confident all along that they would get a commutation, was reported as being calm. Was it because he was a college graduate and had attended law school and understood how the world and the law worked a little better than most prisoners? Or did the thirty-two-year-old former law student just simply have an innate sense of optimism? Did he really believe he would be around to celebrate his thirty-third birthday on June 25, 1938?

Twenty-one-year-old Senauskas was not so sure that either one of them would see May 3, 1938, the day after the pair was scheduled to take their last walk in Rockview. He was only nineteen when he shot Metro Seminuk. By his own testament he had not had a good life. He was used to being in trouble with the law. But did he ever imagine he would be in this much trouble? And for what? —A lousy $200.

April 27 came and went and nothing for the men or the city of Warren had changed but the date. They were still waiting on April 30, when word arrived in Warren from the Board of Pardons secretary Frank R. Hean that their cases would be considered further at the May 24-25 meeting. Hean noted also that because there were so many cases back-logged before the Board, the Board was extending its meetings from one day to two. Meanwhile, they could *relax* and look forward to living at least until Monday, June 6.

Then, on May 23, just one day before the scheduled hearing, Hean contacted Attorney Hampson and informed him that his case would "definitely be disposed of" during the upcoming two days of meetings. Hampson added that Hean informed him that "there would be no further hearing in the case by the Board, but that it would be among those listed for consideration."

All of a sudden things changed in the Warren County Jail. This latest news affected Warren's most notorious jailbirds. Reports stated that even Polens was set back after this latest announcement. One report said that the prisoners were showing more concern than they had after previous announcements and the result of their strain was obvious.

Warren County Jail guards, who had been taking shifts watching the pair twenty-four hours a day, seven days a week reported they were stepping up their vigilance regarding the pair as their fate drew nearer with each day.

On the streets of Warren the atmosphere snapped and popped. Those who believed the men should be put to death were a little surer of their position. After all, if the Board of Pardons was going to let the pair die in the electric chair, after all this time and all their meetings, it surely must be the right decision. On the other hand, those who didn't believe in capital punishment, felt a little less certain the pair would be spared. And those who believed in prayer, prayed: asking only for God's will to put an end to the interminable indecision and spare these two sinners from one more day of torment.

Now communications between Board of Pardons secretary Hean and Attorney Hampson were getting more frequent and more urgent. On Wednesday, May 25, after the second day of the hearings, word reached Warren that the Senauskas-Polens case had not made it before the Board. There were too many cases ahead of it. At this time, the pair had eleven days to live. The tension surrounding the prisoners was ratcheted up to the next level. By this time even the jail guards were getting jumpy.

Then two days later, on May 27, the Associated Press reported that Polens and Senauskas and two other convicted murders had been reprieved yet again. Their Dance with the Devil had been changed from June 6 to July 11. This was the pair's eighth reprieve.

The other lucky prisoners that day were three Italian Immigrants. Cesare Della Valle of Philadelphia had his dance card changed from June 6 to June 11. Della Valle was a former fruit vendor who was convicted of killing the sixteen-year-old daughter of his boarding home keeper while he was on leave from a Civilian Conservation Camp.

Antonio Peronace, of Northumberland, was convicted of killing his wife and father-in-law at Wulpmont. Before coming to America, Peronace was a shepherd boy in Italy.

By now the Board of Pardons was so jammed with cases it had extended its meetings to three days. If a case didn't get heard during the June 27-29 meeting, it most likely wouldn't be decided upon until meetings started again in September. In the meantime, the board reported that Polens and Senauskas had received eight reprieves and it was unlikely that they would get another. It looked to all involved that indeed their day of reckoning was well at hand.

At the same time, a new voice was heard and once again the mysteries of life were further confused by a politician. For reasons known only to him, Governor Earle took up the cause of Roy Lockard of Altoona. (Lockard, it will be recalled, had been convicted of the especially heinous crime of killing a three-year-old toddler by forcing a spike into his skull. He was sentenced to death.) At a press conference, Governor Earle told reporters: "I will continue granting respites to Lockard until my term expires on January 17, 1939. And further, I will go before the pardon board Monday and ask the members to grant the slayer a commutation to life imprisonment."

When asked by a reporter if he was preparing to grant the same clemency to Polens and Senauskas, he responded: "I am not considering similar action in their cases. Their cases are not in the same category as Lockard. Lockard's case is the only one of my administration in which I have taken this action. I would not grant them respites indefinitely unless new evidence warranted."

There is no way to know if Polens and Senauskas ever knew who, besides their attorneys, was their reluctant champion. It is not known how much information Attorney Hampson related to the defendants each time after he returned from Board hearings in Harrisburg. Chances are when Attorney General Margiotti got involved in their case, Hampson may have pointed this out. On the other hand, he may not have. He may have figured that Magiotti was just a name to the prisoners, that there was really no way to impart to them how lucky they were that Margiotti not only had known Attorney MacDonald, but that he had held him in the highest regard possible.

In point of fact Margiotti was on a social and professional strata so far above the prisoners that Hampson might have spoken his name from time to time. But he most likely never attempted to explain just what type of person and what type of personality it takes to rise so high in the legal profession or what the man had done to save their lives.

Margiotti was a well-respected and extremely competent attorney general, and his influence in the case cannot be overstated. Reduced to the simplest terms, one could say that if Margiotti had not got involved in the case the prisoners quite possibly would have already had their Last Dance—months ago.

It was clear that Margiotti attempted to get the Senauskas-Polens case on the June meeting schedule. The reason for this was simple: that June meeting was Margiotti's last. When the Board of Pardons returned to session in September, there would be a new attorney general for the state of Pennsylvania.

On Tuesday, July 5 Governor Earle held a press conference to announce that he had granted Polens and Senauskas their ninth respite. He had moved their execution date to September 26 to allow the new attorney general, Guy K. Bard, sufficient time to acquaint himself with the considerable volume of paperwork that had accumulated in the case.

Meanwhile back in Warren, the Warren County Commissioners decided it was time for them to get involved in the Senauskas-Polens debacle. They didn't like the fact that for over two years the pair had been held in the Warren County Jail and that local taxpayers were footing the considerable bill, not just for their board but for the salaries of the guards who were still posting a death watch around the clock, seven days a week.

The commissioners' plan was to transfer the pair to a regular state prison, such as the one in Erie. They figured that a prison was already staffed around the clock so two more prisoners wouldn't add any unnecessary guard expense. At first, County Commissioner John Lyon would not comment on the plan. But when word reached Warren from Erie County that such an appeal had been made, Lyon stated that the plan had been abandoned.

In their response, Erie County Commissioners Elton Blair and Helen Schluran, told local officials they would accept the prisoners but they would have to charge Warren County the same rate that they charged the federal government. The charge would be 75 cents a day each for food and $12 a day to maintain a death watch. Warren officials were currently paying $15 a day to maintain the around-the-clock guards.

When Warren County Commissioners sent their request to Erie officials they included the fact that "Warren County Jail has only a warden and an assistant on its staff and that should the prisoners escape it would reflect on the men."

In the annals of Warren County's most embarrassing statements ever made by an elected official, the commissioners' above stated quote should certainly rank in the top five. What they're saying is, If these two convicted murderers ever broke out of jail, it would be embarrassing for the warden and his staff. They didn't say that if the prisoners escaped, there would be two desperate killers with nothing to lose and that they posed a serious threat to residents of Warren County.

Aside from the fact that there was a total of five men, presumably trained and with access to weapons if needed, watching the prisoners' every move, these two murderers were physically small men. Senauskas stood 5 foot 9-1/2 and weighed 146 pounds. Polens also stood 5 foot 9 –1/2 but he weighed 192 pounds.

It was not announced whether the Commissioners would give up their attempts to pass the killers off to another prison, but it was rumored that their next plan was to try and have the men shipped to Rockview. But they had not, at that time, received an answer from the warden at Rockview. Whether the county officials liked it or not, while Senauskas and Polens would not be frolicking in the Allegheny River or strolling the avenues, Warren's least favorite sons were going to spend the summer in the Warren County Jail.

When the Board of Pardons met on September 21-22, just four days before the Senauskas and Polens executions were scheduled, it issued four respites. A new name was added to the roster: Fred Holland Mitchell of Somerset County. The other lucky prisoners were Antonio Peronace, Cesare Della Valle, and of course, Warren's own: Joe

Senauskas and John Polens. The Warren pair had their death date changed from Monday, September 26 to Monday, October 31.

This marked the pair's tenth respite.

But just when the men settled in for another month of life, and things in Warren and the Warren County Jail returned to their routine, all hell broke loose. After spending nearly two-and-one-half years in the Warren County Jail, Warren officials learned on Saturday, September 24, that the pair was to be transferred to death row at Rockview State Penitentiary to await their fate with the electric chair.

Warren County Sheriff John P. Berdine received word from the warden at Rockview that he was to deliver the pair to Rockview at noon on Monday, September 26, 1938.

Attorney Harold Hampson visited the men on Sunday and afterward told reporters that despite their move to death row, the men appeared confident their executions would be commuted to life sentences. The pair spent their last Sunday in the Warren County Jail, the same way they had spent each Sunday since they had been incarcerated: they took part in the usual jail service provided by the Salvation Army and afterward each was visited by a spiritual adviser.

At 6 o'clock that Monday morning Sheriff Berdine assembled his contingent of six officers and began the transfer process. There were two state police officers, each driving a state police automobile; these were privates Gordon Foley and George Mazza. Senauskas was assigned to one car and Polens to the other. Also present were Deputy Sheriff William Stuart, Sanford Secor, Sheffield police chief, L.E. Linder, state game protector, and special deputy Ted Berdine, son of Sheriff Berdine.

It didn't take long before the pair realized that life on death row in Rockview was a world apart from their cells in the Warren County Jail. Within a few weeks reality struck the pair hard as one of their own, convicted killer Fred Holland Mitchell, learned that there would be no more respites for him. Mitchell, who had been granted respites along with Senauskas and Polens over the last year, had been convicted of beating his landlady Mary Nash to death with an iron pipe in order to get her husband's clothes.

On his last day, twenty-two-year-old Mitchell, who was an African-American from South Pittsburg, Tennessee, wrote his mother a letter and then slept from 9:30 p.m. to 11:30 p.m. when he was awakened to get ready to meet his maker at 12:30 a.m.

At exactly 12:30 a.m. Monday, Mitchell was strapped into the electric chair and one minute later the electric switch was thrown and three minutes later at 12:34 a.m. he was pronounced dead.

If Polens or Senauskas harbored any lingering doubts about whether their lives were on the line, it must be assumed that Mitchell's execution, just a few feet from their cells, quelled any doubts. It must also be assumed that the men understand beyond any doubt that the Commonwealth of Pennsylvania was capable of inflicting the most serious form of punishment known to man.

In an effort to afford Polens and Senauskas relief from having to witness Mitchell walking past their cells, guards erected screens in front of their cells. The condemned men were spared the otherworldly visage of the young black man shuffling his way into eternity. But nothing could be done to spare them and the others on death row from hearing the hum the electricity sent off as it coursed through Mitchell's body or the smell of burnt flesh. To them, three minutes must have seemed an unmercifully long time.

During the October, 1938 session of the Board of Pardons, which was held on Wednesday and Thursday, October 19-20, the Board announced that two more of Senauskas' and Polens' co-petitioners had their pleas for clemency rejected and were set to be electrocuted. Convicted murder Antonio Peronace would keep his appointment with death as scheduled on Monday, October 31. William Blackwell's appeal was also denied. The African-American from Pittsburgh had his date set for November 7, 1938.

As for the cases of Polens and Senauskas, there was big news reported as the men received an unprecedented eleventh respite, moving their death date forward two months to Monday, January 9, 1939. By now it was becoming obvious that there were some extenuating circumstances in this case that were not being reported. Legal wags from across the state knew something was up in this case. Nobody gets eleven respites.

Finally, on October 20, 1938, an anonymous source told reporters that the reason the Senaukas-Polens matter was taking so long to dispose of was because the Board of Pardons had taken the highly unusual, and in fact unprecedented, step of appealing to the Supreme Court to grant the men new trials. This had never been done before and the source explained that the extra month was tacked on to the respites to give the Supreme Court justices time to see if they could in fact grant the appeal.

As confusing as all of this sounds, there are two plausible explanations. The first explanation was simple: there were board members who didn't believe that Polens and Senauskas deserved the electric chair.

The second explanation was that some or all of the Board members, along with everyone else who came in contact with this case, knew the men were guilty of premeditated murder. And also, enough members of the Board felt that the pair should be executed for their crime. These two facts placed members of the Board in a quandary. The men deserved to die for the murder but, as the last stop on the trail of justice in the Commonwealth, Board members could not sidestep the irrefutable fact that something and perhaps a number of irregular things had happened during their trials. And because of these irregularities the defendants did not receive a fair trial. They were denied due process of law.

The only hope the Board had of moving forward with the executions was to explain this to the Supreme Court and see if some sort of a new statute could be enacted to cover this case and presumably others that might follow. It appeared that members of the Board were confident if this case were to go to trial again, the men would be convicted and sentenced to death.

But that was not going to happen. The Supreme Court had ruled back on March 29, 1938 that it had heard the case three times and it would not hear it again.

As fall turned to winter Senaskas and Polens spent Thanksgiving on death row. And, according to the ruling of the Board of Pardons, they were certain they would have one more Christmas and one more New Year's Eve.

But they were not prepared for what happened to them on the morning of Wednesday, December 14, 1938. Both men were asleep in their cells when Rockview Warden C.W. Rhodes woke them with the news that the Board of Pardons had recommended to Governor Earle that their death sentences be commuted to life imprisonment.

Rhodes told reporters: "They shouted, laughed, and wept at the news. And both agreed it was the best Christmas present anyone could get."

Rhodes read the prisoners the news from the local newspaper and he was quick to point out to the men that their commutation was not official until the governor signed the paperwork. At the time Earle was on vacation and it was not known when he would return to his office in

Harrisburg.

When the news hit the city of Warren there was a mixed reaction. Defense Attorney Harold Hampson had no statement to make but he did say: "I'm just glad the case is finished."

Former District Attorney L.C. Eddy told reporters: "As district attorney I fought the matter to the best of my ability in the interests of the Commonwealth. The procedure was regular from start to finish and vindicates the judge [Arird] of any promise. The decision was theirs [the Board of Pardons] and in the end the men will be punished for their crime."

When asked if he had anything to say former Judge E.S. Lindsey declined comment. Perhaps Judge Lindsey felt that no matter what he said, he couldn't win with this case. Lindsey had a most peculiar role in the case.

If you recall, when the case started out in Judge Arird's court, Lindsey was hired by Arird and the Commonwealth to aid the prosecution. When it came time to vouch for the honesty and integrity of the late Earle V. MacDonald, Lindsey signed an affidavit in favor of MacDonald. Then, when it was time for witnesses to come forward and state that Judge Arird's memory was fine, Lindsey was on the list here as well. And, finally when depositions were taken in the Warren County Courthouse on February 8, 1938 as to what each individual knew, it was Lindsey's deposition that deeply influenced Attorney General Margiotti. Lindsey stated that on the day the men were sentenced Earle MacDonald told him that he had made a deal with Judge Arird.

Comments from other Warren County residents were mixed. A courthouse employee responded, "I expected it and I would feel differently if I were sure they would serve out life terms."

Another resident, a store owner, said, "In view of the other circumstances in the case, I think life is enough."

On December 22, 1938 Governor Earle returned from a three-week vacation in France. Among all the other paperwork that was stacked on his desk, there were one-hundred-and-seventy-five findings of the Board of Pardons for him to act upon before Christmas. Senauskas' and Polens' papers were in that stack. By December 24, Christmas Eve, Earle had pardoned twenty-seven supplicants and modified the sentences of seventy-nine others; but he had not reached the Polens-Senauskas paperwork.

By January 5, 1939 he still had not signed the pair's paperwork. And now it was getting a little dicey for the men. They were scheduled to die on Monday, January 9 at 12:30 a.m. Another day passed and still no word from the governor.

Then, finally, on January 7, 1939 when the pair had just forty-eight hours left to live, Pennsylvania Governor George H. Earle signed the papers, which commuted their death sentences to life in prison.

At a press conference that day, which effectively marked the end of the media attention on this case, Earle told reporters: "They committed a terrible crime, but I do not feel they should go to the electric chair without proper trial by jury."

On Wednesday, January 11, 1939, Joseph Senauskas and John G. Polens were transferred from death row at Rockview State Prison in Bellefonte to Western Penitentiary in Pittsburgh to begin serving their life sentences.

.

EPILOGUE

Mary Seminuk left Warren County shortly after she was released from Muncy. She lived the remainder of her life in Tonawanda, New York, a suburb of Buffalo. She died there in 1989.

John Polens was transferred from Western Penitentiary to Rockview Penitentiary on September 5, 1946. He stayed at Rockview until his sentence was commuted on January 5, 1952. He served thirteen years and twelve days of his life sentence. He was forty-six when he got out. He was on parole for the next ten years; his final discharge was granted July 23, 1962. Polens married and had three stepchildren and three grandchildren. He died in Pittsburgh on November 9, 1976. He is buried in the Good Shepherd Cemetery in Pittsburgh.

Joseph Senauskas was transferred to Rockview State Prison on January 7, 1954. It was rumored that while he was at Western Penitentiary he got in some trouble. It was alleged he was less than an ideal prisoner. This would explain why he was held at Western—a maximum-security unit—eight years more than Polens. In Polens' case, as in most other cases at Western, prisoners who were moving through the system without any problems were reduced from maximum to medium security prior to their release. He had his sentence commuted to minimum parole on February 1, 1957. He served eighteen years, one month, and eight days. He was forty years old when he got out.

After his discharge Senauskas changed his name and moved to

Lansdowne, a suburb of Philadelphia. He married and had two daughters and three grandchildren. He died August 4, 1982 and is buried in Hartford, Connecticut.

APPENDIX A

COMMONWEALTH v. SENAUSKAS
Supreme Court of Pennsylvania
Oct. 8, 1937
1. Criminal law ? 980 (2)

In murder prosecution, assignment that court erred in talking privately with state troopers, deputy sheriff, sheriff, and warden, and in using information so obtained in determining degree of guilt was overruled where conversation of judge with such men related to accused's mental condition, a matter both in issue.
2. Criminal law ? 273

A plea of guilty of murder does not mean a plea of guilty to willful, deliberate, and premeditated murder, but leaves open for judicial determination the degree of guilt, all murder presumed to be of the second degree.
3. Criminal law ? 980 (2)

In murder prosecution, record established that trial judge determined the degree of the offense after plea of guilty, from evidence, as against assignment of error that court erred in its opinion that the plea of guilty included the willful, deliberate, and premeditated killing of the deceased (18 P. S. § 2222).
4. Criminal law ? 980 (2)

Where defendant entered plea of guilty of murder, evidence sustained court's finding that defendant was guilty of murder in the first degree.
5. Criminal law ? 989

Where court, after announcing its decision fixing the degree of murder at first, asking defendant if he had anything to say why sentence should not be pronounced against him, omission of the words "of death" after the word sentence did not constitute reversible error.
6. Criminal law ? 980 1177

Failure of judge to propound to prisoner in capital case inquiry in unequivocal language as to whether he has anything to say why sentence should not be pronounced against him will constitute reversible error only when it is shown that the prisoner has thereby been prejudiced.
7. Criminal law ? 274

In murder prosecution, evidence was insufficient to establish that trial judge made any commitment before plea of guilty was entered as to sentence to be imposed, and justified denial of defendant's request for permission to withdraw plea of guilty.

8. Criminal law ? 274

In hearing on motion for permission to withdraw plea of guilty on ground that trial judge had made commitment before plea was entered as to sentence to be imposed, receiving testimony that defendant previous to trial had expressed an intention to plead guilty was not error.

÷

Appeal No. 242, January term, 1937, from judgement and sentence of Court of Oyer and Terminer, at No.1, June term, 1936; D.U. Arird, President Judge.

Joe Senauskas, alias Joe Sennette, alias Gerald Chapman, was convicted of murder in the first degree, and he appeals.

Affirmed.

Argued before KEPHART, C.J., and SCHAFFER, MAXEY, DREW, LINN, STERN, and BARNES, JJ.

Harold S. Hampson, of Warren, for appellant.

L.C. Eddy, Dist. Atty., of Warren, and Lemuel B. Schofield, Asst. Dist. Atty., of Philadelphia, for the Commonwealth.

MAXEY, Justice.

The appellant, Joe Senauskas, was indicted for the murder of Metro Seminuk. Seminuk and his wife, Mary, lived in Warren County, Pa. He operated a filling station called the "Air Port Inn" on United States Highway Route No. 6, between Youngsville and Pittsfield, and he also conducted there a small grocery store, and sold tobacco and beverages, and maintained a room for dancing. About 12:15 a.m. on March 27, 1936, Seminuk, while standing on the driveway beside his gasoline pump, was shot through the heart, dying almost instantly. He was shot four times. On March 31, 1936, Senauskas was arrested by the state police. At the barracks he admitted complicity in the shooting and showed officers where the revolver was hidden. On April 5, 1936, he made a complete confession in writing. His fingerprints were found on glasses and beer bottles used by him shortly before the shooting at the Air Port Inn. At the time of the homicide his age was 18 years, 4 months, and 6 days.

In his confession he stated that late in the evening of December

31, 1935, he met at a dance in Corry a man named John Polens who asked him if he knew any "racket people," and specifically, "any killers" in Cleveland. A little later Polens told him whom he wanted killed and why. Polens said he wanted the man killed because he (Polens) had lost possession of a farm through this man, and also because he had "defamed him and put the needles to him," as a result of which, Polens, so he claimed, was unable to get a job. A few days later Polens came to see appellant, and the latter told him that he had already gotten in touch with the men in Cleveland and that "they would come and do it" but that they wanted part payment first. Polens then gave appellant $50, but before doing so, he took him to the Air Port Inn and pointed out Seminuk. On March 26, 1936, Polens drove the defendant to take an automobile operator's test for a license. Polens then suggested to Senauskas that they get a car for the latter "to do the job." They went to Buffalo and rented an automobile. On their return they stopped at Youngsville, and Polens produced a revolver and they each "shot into the woods just to see how the gun worked." They then went to Youngsville, where Polens bought a half-pint of whisky and gave it to Senauskas. He also gave appellant $17 "to take the car back with and pay for the use of the car" after the designated victim had been killed. Senauskas said that Polens told him "to give him about an hour's time" to get far enough away so that he could have an alibi. Senauskas states that he finished his half-pint of whisky and then went to the Air Port Inn and asked for "John," which was the name by which Polens had designated Seminuk. He was told that "John" was not there. He then left and went to Corry, where he drank whisky and beer. Defendant later went to the Garland Inn and reported to Polens that he had been to the Air Port Inn and the fellow was not there. Polens told him to "hang around," as the man would be there. He said he drove past the Air Port Inn and then turned around. He stated that the next thing he remembered was when he awoke at 9 a.m. on March 27, 1936. He got into the automobile and went to Garland and made inquiries at Garland as to where Polens lived. The man to whom he made inquiries asked if he (the defendant) was from Warren, remarking that he thought perhaps he had come down to tell Polens "about the shooting they had at the Air Port Inn." This man said someone had shot a man named Metro. Then the defendant stated in his confession: "I got scared and figured I shot the wrong man as the man I was to shoot I knew as John." He later met Polens who gave him $30 and assured him that "Metro and John were the same." Polens later handed Senauskas $120 and told him to leave this part of the country.

Senauskas was called for trial on June 2, 1936. He entered a plea of "not guilty." He was represented by Attorney Earle V. MacDonald, now deceased, which had been appointed counsel by the court. On June 2nd, five jurors had been selected, and on the following morning the defendant in open court asked leave to withdraw his plea of "not guilty" and enter a plea of "guilty." This was granted and the plea entered. The case was continued until June 10, 1936, for the purpose of taking testimony to determine the degree and the sentence.

A hearing was held on June 10th. Defendant's confession and other evidence were received. The presence of Senauskas at the place of the homicide on March 26, 1936, was established by a witness who had talked with him at that place and had left at about 12 o'clock, p.m. when the witness reached a point of about one-hundred-and fifty feet from the inn, he saw the deceased and Senauskas come out of the door and walk around back of the car. He said the defendant got into the car and that he heard the deceased say, "She is full now," and then he saw him take the gasoline hose, walk behind the car, and hang it up on the pump. The deceased then walked to the left-hand side of the car, and immediately the witness heard "three or four shots in rapid succession and a scream at the same time." Immediately the car started out very fast, traveling west without any lights." The witness ran back to the inn and saw Seminuk lying alongside the driveway. He said: "He looked as though he was dead." Another witness also saw the defendant at the Air Port Inn.

The evidence conclusively proved the guilt of Senauskas of murder in the first degree, and on June 23, 1936, in the presence of defendant and his counsel, the court so fixed the degree of murder and imposed the death penalty.

On June 27, 1936, Attorney MacDonald presented to the court a paper entitled "Motion For New Trial And Arrest of Judgment." Permission was asked to withdraw the plea of guilty. No reason of any kind was assigned to support this request. On June 26, 1936, the day before this motion was presented to Judge Arird, Attorney MacDonald presented a petition in the Supreme Court asking leave to withdraw the plea of guilty and for the appointment of another judge to hear the motion for a "new trial." This petition was supported by affidavits to the effect that the guilty plea had been "coerced," in that it was made in response to a promise by Judge Arird that the death penalty would not be imposed. The filing of this petition and the allegations it contained were not made known to Judge Arird, but he learned of it later from the public press.

On September 28, 1936, this court directed James I. Brownson, President Judge of the Twenty-Seventh judicial district, to proceed to Warren county and dispose of the motion filed in the lower court for a new trial, arrest of judgement, and permission to withdraw the plea of guilty, and a little later Judge Brownson was directed to report to this court with respect to the allegations in the petition filed here to the effect that the defendant had changed his plea to guilty upon assurances from Judge Arird that the death penalty would not be imposed. On August 28, 1936, Attorney MacDonald died, and on October 6th next Judge Brownson appointed Harold S. Hampson counsel for Senauskas.

On October 27, 1936, Judge Brownson began a hearing which lasted 5 days. He then reported to the Supreme Court that the allegations in the petition had not been established and that, on the contrary, the evidence clearly "negatived the allegations" of any promises made. The Supreme Court on April 12, 1937 dismissed the petition. On May 7, 1937, an appeal to this court was taken.

There are nine assignments of error. The first assignment is based upon the court's refusal of defendant's motion for a new trial. This assignment is overruled.

[1] The second assignment is as follows: "The court below erred in talking privately with the State Troopers, Deputy Sheriff, Sheriff, and Warden, and in using the information so obtained in determining the degree of guilt of the accused the right to meet with these parties and to be present when they talked concerning him and to cross-examine them regarding their statements." This assignment is based on the following excerpt from the opinion of the court finding the defendant guilty of murder in the first degree: "Now I have talked with the State Troopers, and also the Deputy Sheriff, the ones that arrested Senauskas, and there was no question in their minds but that Senauskas was acting perfectly natural. I have also talked with the Sheriff and the Warden. Nothing wrong with Senauskas except he was a little nervous." It is important to note that the conversation the judge had with these men related to the mental condition of Senauskas, a matter not then nor theretofore raised by appellant

or his counsel. The judge's talk with these men was on a fact not in issue. Therefore, the judgment of guilty of murder in the first degree could not have been based in any measure on any such conversations. The second assignment of error is therefore without merit and is overruled.

[2,3] The third assignment of error is "the court below erred in its opinion and finding that the plea of guilty entered by the defendant included the willful, deliberate and premeditated killing of Metro Seminuk.

While it is not true that a plea of guilty of murder means a plea of guilty to a willful, deliberate, and premeditated murder, for such a plea leaves open for judicial determination the degree of guilt, all murder being presumed to be of the second degree, it is obvious in reading the opinion of Judge Arird in this case that he was familiar with this rule of determination and acted upon it. At the outset he cites the Act of May 14, 1925, P.L. 759 (18 P.S. § 2222), providing, inter alia, as follows: "In cases of pleas of guilty, the court, where it determines the crime to be murder of the first degree, shall at its discretion, impose sentence of death or imprisonment for life." The court then proceeded to review the facts of this case as revealed by the defendant's confession and by witnesses. In the course of his opinion, the judge said: "Senauskas used a deadly weapon against a vital part of the body, i.e., a shot passed through the heart of Seminuk. Under such circumstances we have a right to presume that malice and intention existed. Senauskas not only had ample time while sitting in this Inn to deliberate and premeditate, but under his own statements the arrangements between him and Polens had been going on for several days, if not weeks. The conclusion of the court states "after the examination of witnesses and hearing had in due form of law * * * adjudged and determined that the crime and the degree of the crime whereof the said Joe Senauskas * * * is convicted by his own plea of guilty and his confession and testimony taken, is murder in the first degree." The third assignment of error is overruled.

[4] The fourth assignment is that "the court below erred in finding the defendant guilty of murder in the first degree." It is overruled.

The fifth assignment is based on the sentence. It is overruled.

[5] The sixth assignment is based on the failure of the judge "to ask the defendant, prior to the imposition of sentence, if he had anything to say why sentence of death should not be pronounced against him." The record shows that, after the court announced its decision fixing the degree

of murder at first, it asked the defendant, "Have you anything to say why sentence should not be pronounced against you?" Appellant contends that this is error because the question did not contain the words "of death" after the word "sentence."

Blackstone in volume 4, page 376, in referring to this traditional inquiry, states that the prisoner should be asked "if he has anything to say why judgement should not be awarded against him." In Rizzolo v. Com. 126 Pa. 54, 17 A. 520, 521, before imposing the death sentence on a defendant convicted of murder in the first degree, the prisoner was called to the bar and asked if he had "anything to say why sentence should not be pronounced against him." This was held sufficient to sustain judgement. In that case the Supreme Court in an opinion by Chief Justice Paxson, said: "As no sentence was possible but that of death, we think there was no omission." It is true that now, when a man is adjudged guilty of murder in the first degree, there remains a choice of two possible sentences to be imposed, these being death or life imprisonment. However, even under the law as it now stands, we think that, when a defendant convicted of murder in the first degree is addressed as was the prisoner at bar, the omission of the words "of death" does not constitute reversible error.

The rule of common law as to the right of the prisoner to be asked whether he had anything to say why judgement should not be awarded against him or, to put it another way, why sentence of death should not be pronounced against him, does not now possess the inflexibility it did in an earlier day. At common law the rule served a purpose that could not be served in any other way. It gave a prisoner in a capital case "an opportunity to allege any ground or arrest, or to plead a pardon, if he had obtained one, or so urge any other legal objection to further proceedings against him." Schwab v. Bergren, 143 U.S. 442, 446, 12 S. Ct. 525, 526, 36 L. Ed. 218. Putting this question to the prisoner gave him his last opportunity to speak to someone with power to save him from his impending doom. To deprive him of this last opportunity was a serious invasion of his rights, for at common law the defendant in cases of felony was not afforded the privilege of counsel nor could he take any appeal to a higher court. A sentence of death in Pennsylvania has no such irrevocability about it as it had at common law. Anything Senauskas could have said before sentence was imposed, he could by himself or counsel have said since with equal effect, either to Judge Arird, Judge Brownson, or to this court.

[6] Modern criminal procedure has thus taken away this rule's *raison d'etre,* and it is an honored maxim of the law that *"cessante ratione legis cessat, et ipsa lex."*[6] However, the practice of propounding to a prisoner in a capital case the above-stated question has long been followed, and since, as Chief Justice Gibson once said (Hamilton v. Com., 16 Pa. 129, 134), "forms of records are deeply seated in the foundations of law," careful judges will continue to make in such cases this ancient inquiry in unequivocal language. Failure to do so will constitute reversible error only when it is shown that the prisoner has been thereby prejudiced.

In Hamilton v. Co., Pa. 129, 133, 55 Am.Dec. 485, the Supreme Court, in an opinion by Chief Justice Gibson, said: "The premises to found a sentence of death are set forth in 1 Chitty's Crim. Law 720, and the form of the entire record is given in 4 Black. Com. Ap. 1" In that case the error alleged was "the omission to place upon the record the inquiry made to the prisoner after conviction if he knows or hath anything to say for himself why the commonwealth should ought not to proceed to judgement," etc. This court held that "there is nothing on the docket to show even that the prisoner was present when he was sentenced, except the supplemental memorandum that 'he was present in court during every stage of the trial, from the time of his arraignment up to the time when the sentence was passed by the honorable Ellis Lewis, president judge of the court, on him.'" The judgement was reversed and the prisoner discharged. The record in the case at bar presents no such fatal omission.

In Gannon v. People, 127 Ill. 507, 21 N.E. 525, 529, 11 Am.St.Rep. 147, the Supreme Court of Illinois held that, "while it is better to call upon the defendant to say why he should not be sentenced, yet the omission to do so is no ground for reversal in any case * * * a motion may be made in arrest of judgement. Under our system, the motion in arrest and the motion for a new trial are disposed of before the time for the sentence arrives." In Sarah v. State 28 Ga. 576, the Supreme court of Georgia held that such failure to ask the accused "if [she] have anything to say why sentence should not be pronounced, is not such an irregularity as will entitle the accused to a new trial." There Judge Lumpkin said: "The ancient practice was for the court to call on the prisoner, if he or she had anything to say why sentence should not be passed. It originated at a time when prisoners were not allowed the benefit of counsel and when the court was counsel to the prisoner, so far as to see that he was deprived of no legal right. Besides the benefit of clergy was also allowed; and at this stage it was claimed." The ruling in that case was upheld in Steel v. State, 149 Ga. 134, 99 S.E. 305, 307, where the Supreme Court of Georgia said: "If the defendant had been deprived of any substantial right by failure of the court to ask the question, or had the court refused to hear from the accused or his counsel on some meritorious objection to his passing sentence, another question might be raised. But that is not this case. On the contrary, a motion in arrest of judgement was made in the case. What more could the question, if asked, have accomplished? The law will not require a vain thing to be done, and will not remand a case where no error or injury has been shown."[7] The sixth assignment of error is overruled.

[7] The seventh assignment is based on the refusal of the court to permit the defendant to withdraw his plea of guilty. In Com. V. Senauskas, 326 Pa. 69, 191 A. 167, 168, this court, in an opinion by the present Chief Justice, reviewed the question of the alleged "bargain" made by the judge not to impose the death penalty in this case. In the opinion appears the following: "It may be stated generally that for a judge to make a bargain, engagement, or promise in advance of the hearing of the case, irrespective of what the evidence might thereafter show the facts to be and as to what judgement he should render therein, would be judicial misconduct." This court said further: "allegations of such misconduct should be clearly proved to warrant fastening of discredit upon any judicial officer. In the instant case, as President Judge Brownson found, the evidence negatives the existence of any improper conduct on the part of the presiding judge. A host of witnesses supported Judge Arird's assertion that no promise had been made. Indeed, defendant had indicated before the trial that he intended to plead guilty and trust to the leniency of the court. * * * If a defendant is aggrieved by the action of the court, the imposition of the death penalty, the overruling of the motion for a new trial, or any other matter, or decree, or judgement, he may take his appeal to this court, the only procedure by which this entire record may be removed here and reconsidered. We will consider at that time all matters connected therewith. The testimony which was heard by Judge Brownson upon the present motion will be considered as part of the record to be reviewed by us."

The burden of proving that Judge Arird made any commitment

before the plea of guilty was entered, as to the sentence to be imposed, was not sustained. The presumption is that it was not made. Regardless of the presumption in favor of the regularity and propriety of official conduct, the allegation is *prima facie* incredible, for there was no motive for such commitment; the evidence then available showed that the Commonwealth was justified in asking for a conviction of the defendant of the highest degree of murder and for the imposition of the extreme penalty.

The only admissible evidence to support the burden of proof is the testimony of A.L. Cohen, Polen's Attorney, who testified that he said (addressing Judge Arird at the time of trial): "I have just talked to Mr. MacDonald and he has told me he is going to enter a plea. Will you give me the same consideration as you do Mr. MacDonald?" The judge replied, according to Mr. Cohen: "I will give you every consideration; of course. I will give you the consideration I will give Mr. MacDonald or anybody else that comes into this court." Attorney Cohen admitted on cross-examination that Judge Arird made him no promises.

Attorney MacDonald, now deceased made an ex parte affidavit on June 25, 1936 that on June 3rd, Judge Arird sent for him before court opened and promised him on his own volition that "if a plea of guilty was entered [for Senauskas], the penalty would not be the electric chair," and that the plea of guilty that day entered in open court "was upon the advice of deponent as counsel upon the representation of the Court that the sentence would not be, in case of first degree murder being found, the electric chair," and that "he communicated the facts relating to the conversation to A.L. Cohen, Esq., who represented John G. Polens."

Judge Arird's version of what happened is that at 9:30 a.m., on the second day of trial, Attorney MacDonald came into his chambers and talked with him in the presence of the court stenographer. The attorney stated that he was nervous and wanted the judge to tell him how to proceed with the case. The judge refused to do so. The attorney then said that his client was "clearly guilty" and that he intended to advise him to plead guilty. To this Judge Arird replied that Mr. MacDonald should use his own judgement. "There was no other discussion of any kind." Nothing was said as to the sentence to be imposed. Court was then opened and defendant and his counsel came to the bar. Leave was asked to withdraw the plea of not guilty and to enter a plea of guilty. The court asked the appellant if he desired to withdraw his plea and enter a plea of guilty "and the defendant replied in the affirmative."

The record completely supports Judge Brownson's conclusion that the plea of guilty entered in this case was not induced by any promise made by him that the death penalty would not be imposed. This assignment of error is overruled.

[8] The eighth assignment of error is based upon the alleged error of Judge Brownson in receiving testimony that the defendant, previous to trial had expressed an intention to plead guilty. This assignment is overruled.

The ninth assignment of error is based on the alleged error of the court below in approving L.B. Schofield, Esq., as assistant district attorney. This assignment is overruled.

The judgement of the court below is affirmed, and the record is remitted so that sentence may be carried out.

***

COMMONWEALTH v. POLENS
Supreme Court of Pennsylvania
Oct. 8, 1937
1. Criminal law ? 988

Where counsel of defendant who had entered plea of guilty in murder prosecution was present when hearing was had to elicit facts for determination of degree of defendant's guilt, and appropriate penalty, and where record proved beyond all reasonable doubt that defendant was guilty of murder in the first degree, fact that the defendant was sentenced during his counsel's absence was not reversible error, since no harm to defendant resulted therefrom.
2. Criminal law ? 988

The practice of sentencing a defendant in the absence of his counsel is condemned.
3. Criminal law ? 980 (2)

When a defendant pleads guilty to charge of murder, he submits his fate to the court to which his plea is addressed, and he is then entitled to have the court proceed in the prescribed form and with proper regard to rules of law and evidence to elicit facts for determination of degree of his guilt and appropriate penalty.

÷

Appeal No. 223, January term, from the judgement and sentence of court of Oyer and Terminer, Warren County, at No. 2 June term, 1936;

D.U. Arird, President Judge.

John G. Polens was convicted of murder, and he appeals.

Affirmed.

Argued before KEPHART, C.J., AND SCHAFFER, MAXEY, DREW, LINN, STERN, AND BARNES, JJ.

A. Lincoln Cohen, of Pittsburgh, and Samuel J. Goldstein, of McKeesport, for appellant.

L.C. Eddy, Dist. Atty., of Warren, and Lemuel B. Schofield, Asst. Dist. Atty., of Philadelphia, for the Commonwealth.

MAXEY, Justice

The appellant, John G. Polens, was indicted for the murder of Metro Seminuk. The facts of this homicide are set forth in the opinion which was filed in the case of Commonwealth v. Joseph Senauskas, Polens' codefendant. (Pa. Sup.) 194 A. 646, and need not be repeated here. Polens confessed his guilt, and his confession is in accord with that of Senauskas on all material matters. At the time of the commission of the murder, Polens was nearly 31 years of age. He was a graduate of an academy in Pittsburgh. He later took a two-year course in science and a four-year course in business administration. He obtained the degree of bachelor of economics in 1927 and attended a law school for two years. He served by appointment as justice of the peace in Pittsfield Township, Warren County. His term expired in January, 1936, and he was an unsuccessful candidate for that office. He admitted in his confession that he was friendly with Mary Seminuk, wife of the victim named in the indictment. He said: "On many occasions I went on certain trips with her in order to help her conduct her business." He disclosed no intimacy with her. He admitted that he had animosity toward Seminuk because of his (Polens') "frustrated attempts at office" and other matters which in his "own imagination" he blamed Seminuk for. He admitted that he had paid money to Senauskas both before and after the homicide, the last payment being in the sum of $120, that he knew of Senauskas' intention to kill Seminuk, and that he had given Senauskas the revolver with which the shooting was done.

Counsel for Polens presented a petition for the appointment of a psychiatrist to examine the prisoner. The petition was granted. The appointee, Dr. R.H. Israel, superintendent of Warren County State Hospital, reported that Polens "appeared to be above the average in intellectual ability, fully aware of the nature of his acts and the consequences thereof, and there is no reason to believe that he has reacted as the result of hallucinations or insane motives."

When appellant was called for trial and arraigned, he pleaded guilty. The case was continued until June 12, 1936, for the purpose of taking testimony to fix the degree of guilt and the punishment. At the hearing on June 12th, Polens' confession was not repudiated by him nor attacked in any way.

In his argument in this case appellant's counsel stresses the assignment of errors which are practically identical with the second, third, sixth, and seventh assuagements of error in the Senauskas Case. What we have said in discussing those four assignments in our opinion in that case may be treated as a part of the opinion in this case, and no further discussion is required.

[1,2] Appellant's counsel also stresses an assignment of error based upon the fact that when Polens was sentenced his counsel was not present. On the date fixed for sentencing Polens, his counsel telegraphed the court that he was unable to be present. The court, however, did not defer sentence. While the practice of sentencing a defendant in the absence of his counsel is most unusual and is hereby condemned, we do not hold that counsel's absence in this case constitutes reversible error, no harm to defendant having resulted therefrom. Counsel was present when the hearing was had to elicit facts for the determination of defendant's guilt and the appropriate penalty.

[3] The record in this case proves beyond all reasonable doubt that the appellant was guilty of murder in the first degree and that a just penalty was imposed. Senauskas was the "trigger man"; he was the "hand and tool" for the homicide, but Polens was the brain by which the "hand and tool" was guided and directed. In view of the appellant's plea of guilty, made without any inducement or promise, no further duty confronted the court except to determine the degree of guilt and to fix the penalty. When a defendant pleads guilty to a charge of murder, he submits his fate to the court to which his plea is addressed. He is then entitled to have the court proceed in the prescribed form and with proper regards to the rules and law and evidence to elicit facts for the scales of justices in which his guilt is weighed. In the performance of its duty in this respect, the court did not substantially depart from the bounds of "due process."

The competent evidence received at the hearing amply sustained the court's finding and warranted the penalty imposed.

None of the assignments of error in this case require discussion except those we have referred to, and these have been discussed in the opinion this day filed in the Senauskas Case, and which discussion is by express reference incorporated in this opinion.

All the assignments of error are overruled.

FOOTNOTES

[1] As to the location of the death penalty: It's unclear why Judge Arird sentenced Senauskas to death at Western Penitentiary, which was located in Pittsburgh. Since 1915 all executions by electrocution in Pennsylvania have been administered at Rockview State Prison in Centre County. Researching the Pennsylvania Department of Corrections historical files, the prison in Centre County is referred to as "the new Western Penitentiary in Centre County" in one publication and the "New Central Penitentiary in Centre County" in another. In yet another reference, Rockview was referred to as being built as a medium-security facility in 1912 to alleviate overcrowded conditions at Western, and therefore it could have been regarded as an extension or a branch of Western. But clearly, by 1936, there had been dozens of electrocutions at Rockview and it must be assumed that everyone involved in Pennsylvania's criminal justice system knew where executions took place. So, did Judge Arird err when he set the death sentence at Western? Did he not know that since the first death by electrocution in 1915 all death sentences were carried out at Rockview? One explanation could be that Judge Arird simply had no knowledge of the how and the why and the wherefore of the death penalty: he had been involved in only two death penalty cases in his career. The first case being when he was an attorney for John Andrews, who was accused and convicted of murder in Warren in 1912, which is referred to in Chapter III of this book. It must be pointed out that in 1912 death sentences were administered by hanging at the prison where the defendant was housed. Is it possible that a judge could not know this? Or is it more realistic to assume that it was not an error at all, but merely the fault of the PADOC for not clearly naming its prisons? Or was it just an oversight that nobody, including the defense attorneys, caught? It's unlikely we'll ever know the truth.

[2] The terms tipstaff and a court crier are still used today, as is the modern term bailiff.

[3] Bruno Hauptman was convicted of the 1932 kidnapping and murder of Charles Lindbergh's twenty-two-month-old son, Charles, Jr. Hauptman was executed April 6, 1936.

4 *Nunc pro tunc* means "now for then." Indicates action in the present in place of an action that should have been taken before.

5 *Certiorari* means "to be informed of." It is also the name given to certain appellate proceedings for reexamination of actions of a trial court or inferior appeals court.

6 Where the reason for the existence of a law ceases, the law itself should also cease. The maxim means that no common-law rule can survive the reasons on which it is founded. It needs no statute to change it; it abrogates itself. If the reasons on which a law rests are overborne by opposing reasons, which, in the progress of society, gain controlling force, the old law though still good as an abstract principle, and good in its application to some circumstances, must cease to apply or to be a controlling principle to the new circumstances. Beardsley v Hartford, 50 Conn 542.

7 In a letter dated August 17, 1937, the Master of the Crown Office and Registrar of Criminal appeal of England, informed the writer that the question herein discussed is invariably asked in England of all prisoners before sentence in capital cases, but there is no statutory requirement that this question must be asked. That official expressed his opinion as follows: "If such an objection was raised it would be brushed aside by the court of Criminal Appeal, but of course I speak under correction."